OFF THE GROUND

AN ANTHOLOGY OF POETRY

Compiled by

WILLIAM KERR, M.A.

LATE

DIRECTOR OF STUDIES, THE TRAINING COLLEGE, GLASGOW

Author of "The English Apprentice"

and

ALEXANDER HADDOW, B.A.

LATE

PRINCIPAL MASTER OF METHOD, THE TRAINING COLLEGE, GLASGOW

*Author of "On the Teaching of Poetry" and "The Ring and the
Book as a Connected Narrative"*

BOOK I

Granger Index Reprint Series

BOOKS FOR LIBRARIES PRESS

FREEPORT, NEW YORK

STANDARD BOOK NUMBER:
8369-6067-X

LIBRARY OF CONGRESS CATALOG CARD NUMBER:
76-75516

PREFACE

" Poesy only instructs as it delights."—*John Dryden.*

" The end of writing is to instruct; the end of poetry is to instruct by pleasing."—*Samuel Johnson.*

Those sentences, we hope, are an indication at once of the purpose and the plan of this anthology. In making it we have been guided by one consideration—the aesthetic value of each poem for the readers we have in view. Of our notes we would merely say what will be immediately obvious, that we have made no attempt to construct lessons. We believe, indeed, that for every poem taught many should be read aloud, and that very often a beautiful and sympathetic reading will teach more than all the commentators. Naturally, therefore, we hold that no book can take the place of the teacher, whose ultimate aim is to lead pupils to enjoy reading poetry for themselves.

W. K.
A. H.

Publishers' Note

This book has been prepared in collaboration, but Mr. Kerr has the final responsibility for the selection as a whole, and for the discussion of poems on pages 10-52, while Mr. Haddow has the final responsibility for the discussion of poems on pages 53-85.

ACKNOWLEDGMENTS

We value highly the permission to include copyright material in this anthology, and are happy to put on record our indebtedness for :

" GALLOPING DICK " to Miss Almey St. John Adcock.

PASSAGE from " ALARMS AND EXCURSIONS ", by Lieut.-Gen. Sir Tom Bridges, K.C.B., K.C.M.G.. D.S.O., to Messrs. Longmans Green & Co.

" THE LITTLE YOUNG LAMBS " to Mr. Patrick Chalmers.

" PUK-WUDJIES " and " SOLOMON AND THE MONKEYS " to Mr. Patrick Chalmers and Messrs. Methuen & Co., Ltd., Publishers of " Green Days and Blue Days ".

" THE TORTOISESHELL CAT " to Mr. Patrick Chalmers and Messrs. Methuen & Co., Ltd., Publishers of " A Peck o' Maut ".

" THE FOX CUB " to the Editor of " Country Life ".

" THE TRAIN " to the Executors of Sir Henry Newbolt and Messrs. Elkin Matthews and Marrot, Publishers of " Poems " by Mary Coleridge.

" GRIM ", " OFF THE GROUND ", " SAM ", and " THE HORSEMAN " to Mr. Walter de la Mare. Reprinted from " Collected Poems " published by Messrs. Constable & Co.

" THE VAGABOND " and " THE BLACKBIRD " to the Author's Representatives, and Messrs. Sidgwick & Jackson, Publishers of " Collected Poems " by John Drinkwater.

" THE GLASS SHIP ", reprinted from " Punch ", by permission of the Proprietors and Miss Rose Fyleman.

" ON A CAT, AGEING " to Messrs. Faber & Faber.

" WHAT THE WEATHER DOES " to Messrs. Blackie & Son, Ltd.

" EDDI'S SERVICE " to Mrs. Rudyard Kipling and Messrs. MacMillan & Co., Publishers of " Rewards and Fairies ".

" ROAD SONG OF THE BANDAR-LOG " to Mrs. Rudyard Kipling and Messrs. MacMillan & Co., Publishers of " The Jungle Book ".

" SONG OF THE BROWN SEA RAT " to Mr. Hamish MacLaren and Messrs. Victor Gollancz, Ltd.

" ST MARY'S BELLS ", " THE TARRY BUCCANEER ", and " CARGOES ", reprinted from " Collected Poems of John Masefield " (William Heinemann, Ltd.) by permission of the Author.

" THE FROZEN OCEAN " to Miss Viola Meynell.

" THE FIDDLE " to the Author's Trustees and Messrs. Wm. Blackwood & Sons, Ltd., Publishers of " The Poetry of Neil Munro ".

" THE TOY BAND " to the Author's Executors and Mr. John Murray, Publisher of " Poems New and Old " by Sir Henry Newbolt.

" COUNTRY BUSES " by Mr. W. H. Ogilvie, to the Proprietors of " Punch ".

" A CHRISTMAS CAROL " to the Author's Representatives and Messrs. MacMillan & Co., Ltd., Publishers of " The Poetical Works of Christina Rossetti ".

" A BIT OF COLOUR " to Mr. Nowell Smith and The Oxford University Press.

" BLUE STARS AND GOLD " to Mr. James Stephens and Messrs. MacMillan & Co., Ltd., Publishers of " Collected Poems " by James Stephens.

" FROM A RAILWAY CARRIAGE ", reprinted from " A Child's Garden of Verses " (Robert Louis Stevenson) by permission of Mr. Lloyd Osbourne.

" GOLLYWOG " by Miss Jan Struther, to the Proprietors of " Punch ".

CONTENTS

		POEM	NOTES
To Each and Every Reader		9	
Off the Ground		10	87
The Fiddle		14	88
St Mary's Bells		16	90
The Minstrel at the Gate		17	91
The Toy Band		20	92
The Retreat from Mons		21	93
The Knight's Leap		24	95
Leezie Lindsay		26	96
Allen-a-Dale		26	96
My Lady Greensleeves		28	98
The Wee Wee Man		30	99
Puk-Wudjies		32	100
Grim		34	102
The Horseman		34	102
Three Charms		35	102
Galloping Dick		36	103
The Fox-cub		38	104
The Tortoiseshell Cat		39	105
On a Cat, Ageing		40	106
Old Winter		41	106
Eddi's Service		42	108
A Christmas Carol		44	108
The Frozen Ocean		45	109
The Little Young Lambs		46	110
A Bit of Colour		48	111

		POEM	NOTES
What the Weather Does		49	111
The Blackbird		50	112
The Glass Ship		51	112
Blue Stars and Gold		52	113
Country Buses		53	114
From a Railway Carriage		55	115
The Train		56	116
Border March		57	117
The Song of the Western Men		58	118
Song of the Brown Sea Rat		59	119
Sam		62	120
The Lowlands of Holland		64	121
The Tarry Buccaneer		65	122
The Vagabond		66	122
Hie Away		67	123
In Summer Time		68	124
Cargoes		69	124
Solomon and the Monkeys		70	126
Road-song of the Bandar-log		72	127
Gollywog		73	127
A Miraculous Passage in Hamelen		74	—
The Legend of the Pied Piper		75	—
The Pied Piper of Hamelin		77	128

PAGES

INDEX OF AUTHORS

		Page
Anonymous	In Summer Time	68
	Leezie Lindsay	26
	My Lady Greensleeves	28
	The Lowlands of Holland	64
	The Wee Wee Man	30
Adcock, Almey St. John	Galloping Dick	36
Bridges, Sir Tom	The Retreat from Mons	21
Browning, Robert	The Pied Piper of Hamelin	77
Chalmers, Patrick	Puk-Wudjies	32
	Solomon and the Monkeys	70
	The Little Young Lambs	46
	The Tortoiseshell Cat	39
Cole, Hylda	The Fox-cub	38
Coleridge, Mary	The Train.	56
De La Mare, Walter	Grim	34
	Off the Ground	10
	Sam	62
	The Horseman,	34
Drinkwater, John	The Blackbird	50
	The Vagabond	66
Fyleman, Rose	The Glass Ship	51
Gray, Alexander	On a Cat, Ageing	40
Hawker, Robert	The Song of the Western Men	58
Hendry, Hamish	What the Weather Does	49
Herrick, Robert	Three Charms	35
Howell, James	A Miraculous Passage in Hamelen	74
Kingsley, Charles	The Knight's Leap	24
Kipling, Rudyard	Eddi's Service	42
	Road-song of the Bandar-log	72
Maclaren, Hamish	Song of the Brown Sea Rat	59
Masefield, John	Cargoes	69
	St Mary's Bells	16
	The Tarry Buccaneer	65

		Page
Meynell, Viola	The Frozen Ocean	45
Munro, Neil	The Fiddle	14
Newbolt, Henry	The Toy Band	20
Noel, Thomas	Old Winter	41
Ogilvie, Will. H.	Country Buses.	53
Rossetti, Christina	A Christmas Carol	44
Scott, Sir Walter	Allen-a-Dale	26
	Border March	57
	Hie Away	67
	The Minstrel at the Gate	17
Smith, Horace	A Bit of Colour	48
Stephens, James	Blue Stars and Gold	52
Stevenson, Robert Louis	From a Railway Carriage	55
Struther, Jan	Gollywog	73

OFF THE GROUND

TO EACH AND EVERY READER

As you read Mr. de la Mare's poem overleaf, you will discover at least two excellent reasons for its title. But perhaps you may wonder why the name of one poem has been given to the whole book. It is because poetry, of all kinds of writing, is best able to lift its readers " off the ground ", off the ordinary ground of humdrum, everyday life, up into new, wonderful, and beautiful worlds.

Read " The Fiddle " (page 14) " The Wee Wee Man " (page 30) and " Sam " (page 62). At once you find yourself in lands of magic, leading the Elfin People over the hills and far away, riding to a bonny hall with roof of gold and floor of crystal, listening to a mermaid singing in " the solitudinous sea ". Read " The Toy Band " (page 20) " The Knight's Leap " (page 24) " The Song of the Western Men " (page 58) and you are in another new land, of courage and fine, brave deeds where men act as you would like to do, and triumph over difficulties, even over death itself. Or read " The Glass Ship " (page 51) " Blue Stars and Gold " (page 52) " The Train " (page 56) and learn how poets can write about quite ordinary things and make you look at them in such a way that they become more strange and beautiful than ever you had thought them to be.

His two companions told Farmer Turvey (page 13) that he had danced them off the ground. Poets have the same power. We are swept off the ground by the speed of " Galloping Dick " (page 36). We jump and skip with " The Little Young Lambs " (page 46). We dance to the tune of " What the Weather Does " (page 49) or to that of " In Summer Time " (page 68). To the " Song of the Brown Sea Rat " we shout, " Ho ho ho, and a ho once again " (page 60).

There are many other new worlds in this book, some easy to enter, some more difficult, many bright and full of colour, a few quiet and grey, all beautiful. Read the poems as well as you can and you will find the upward roads are open before you. Now and again the questions and notes may help to show you the way.

OFF THE GROUND

Three jolly Farmers
Once bet a pound
Each dance the others would
Off the ground.
Out of their coats   5
They slipped right soon,
And neat and nicesome
Put each his shoon.
One-Two-Three !
And away they go,   10
Not too fast,
And not too slow ;
Out from the elm-tree's
Noonday shadow,
Into the sun   15
And across the meadow.
Past the schoolroom,
With knees well bent,
Fingers a-flicking,
They dancing went.   20
Up sides and over,
And round and round,
They crossed click-clacking
The Parish bound ;
By Tupman's meadow   25
They did their mile,
Tee-to-tum
On a three-barred stile.
Then straight through Whipham,
Downhill to Week,   30
Footing it lightsome,
But not too quick,

Up fields to Watchet,
And on through Wye,
Till seven fine churches   35
They'd seen skip by—
Seven fine churches,
And five old mills,
Farms in the valley,
And sheep on the hills;   40
Old Man's Acre
And Dead Man's Pool
All left behind,
As they danced through Wool.
And Wool gone by,   45
Like tops that seem
To spin in sleep
They danced in dream:
Withy—Wellover—
Wassop—Wo—   50
Like an old clock
Their heels did go.
A league and a league
And a league they went,
And not one weary,   55
And not one spent.
And lo, and behold!
Past Willow-cum-Leigh
Stretched with its waters
The great green sea.   60
Says Farmer Bates,
" I puffs and I blows,
What's under the water,
Why, no man knows! "
Says Farmer Giles,   65
" My wind comes weak,
And a good man drownded
Is far to seek."

But Farmer Turvey,
On twirling toes,
Up's with his gaiters,
And in he goes :
Down where the mermaids
Pluck and play
On their twangling harps
In a sea-green day ;
Down where the mermaids,
Finned and fair,
Sleek with their combs
Their yellow hair. . . .
Bates and Giles
On the shingle sat,
Gazing at Turvey's
Floating hat.
But never a ripple
Nor bubble told
Where he was supping
Off plates of gold.
Never an echo
Rilled through the sea
Of the feasting and dancing
And minstrelsy.
They called—called—called :
Came no reply :
Nought but the ripples'
Sandy sigh.
Then glum and silent
They sat instead,
Vacantly brooding
On home and bed,
Till both together
Stood up and said :

" Us knows not, dreams not,
Where you be,
Turvey, unless
In the deep blue sea ;
But axcusing silver—
And it comes most willing—
Here's us two paying
Our forty shilling ;
For it's sartin sure, Turvey,
Safe and sound,
You danced us square, Turvey,
Off the ground ! "

105

110

WALTER DE LA MARE
(20th Century)

1. Was it necessary that the poet should actually tell us those were " jolly " farmers ? Should we have lost anything had he written " Three neighbour farmers " ?

2. Would Farmer Turvey be happy under the sea ?

3. Did he ever come back to his friends ?

4. On what kind of day did they dance ?

5. Was it a quick dance or a slow one ? Which lines tell us ?

6. *Three jolly Farmers once bet a pound*
   Each dance the others would off the ground.
   Out of their coats they slipped right soon,
   And neat and nicesome put each his shoon.

   If the poem had been set out in long lines like this, should we have enjoyed it as much as we do ?

7. How shall we read the poem ?

8. Is " Off The Ground " a good title for it ?

Notes : page 87.

THE FIDDLE

When I was young, I had no sense,
I bought a fiddle for eighteenpence,
And the only tune that I could play,
Was Over The Hills and Far Away.

To learn another I had no care,   5
For oh ! it was a bonny air,
And all the wee things of the glen
Came out and gathered round me then.

The furry folk that dwell in wood
Quitted their hushed green solitude,   10
Came round about me, unafraid,
And skipped to the music that I made.

Birds of the moor, birds of the tree
Took up the tune with fiddle and me ;
Happy were we on that summer day   15
With Over The Hills and Far Away.

I hied me up on the lone hill road
Where the Little Green People have their abode,
And fiddled to them on the ruined cairn
Till they all came out from the rush and fern.   20

With gossamer threads the fields were laid,
That shimmered like silk where the sunlight played,
Quick over them hurried the fairy throng
And danced to the strains of the darling song.

Their gowns were made of the linnet's feather,   25
Their hats of the purple bells of heather,
And oh ! how they chuckled with elfin glee
To the zig-a-zig-zig of my minstrelsy !

'Twas I was the Captain of that band
That played with me in fairy land, 30
Till the moon leaned over the hills to stare,
And see who fiddled the fairy air.

Fr-r-rip !—the furry folk turned and fled,
And every bird to the thicket sped.
In a flash my fairy friends were gone, 35
And fiddle and I were all alone.

I sold my fiddle to buy a drum,
But never again did the fairies come,
And all the bliss of that happy day
Is Over The Hills and Far Away. 40

NEIL MUNRO
(*20th Century*)

1. The first stanza is an old rhyme known to us all. It has delighted the poet so much that it has led him to make from it the story he tells in lines 5-40.

    (*a*) What line in the first stanza gave him most of all the idea for his poem ?

    (*b*) What else did the first stanza give him ? You may find the answer in stanza 2.

2. What does the poet tell us about the tune the fiddle played ?

3. Read again lines 25-28. Do you say

$$\overset{\prime}{zi}g\text{-}a\text{-}\overset{\prime}{zig}\text{-}zig \quad \text{or} \quad zig\text{-}a\text{-}\overset{\prime}{zi}g\text{-}\overset{\prime}{zig} ?$$

4. Would the Three Jolly Farmers dance to this fiddle's tune ?

5. Try to make a picture of the fiddler and his friends.

6. Why does the poet repeat the line,

    Over The Hills and Far Away ?

7. Is this an " Off The Ground " poem ?

    Notes : page 88.

ST MARY'S BELLS

It's pleasant in Holy Mary
By San Marie lagoon,
The bells they chime and jingle
From dawn to afternoon.
They rhyme and chime and mingle,
They pulse and boom and beat,
And the laughing bells are gentle
And the mournful bells are sweet.

Oh, who are the men that ring them,
The bells of San Marie,
Oh, who but sonsie seamen
Come in from over sea,
And merrily in the belfries
They rock and sway and hale,
And send the bells a-jangle,
And down the lusty ale.

It's pleasant in Holy Mary
To hear the beaten bells
Come booming into music,
Which throbs, and clangs, and swells,
From sunset till the daybreak,
From dawn to afternoon,
In port of Holy Mary
On San Marie lagoon.

JOHN MASEFIELD
(20*th Century*)

lagoon : *a shallow channel protected from the force of the sea*
sonsie : *cheerful, hearty*   lusty : *strong*

1. Why is it pleasant in Holy Mary ?
2. Mark other words in the poem like " chime " and " jingle "
   that are commonly used to describe the sound of bells.
3. By what other ways has the poet made us hear the music of
   bells ?
4. Read aloud lines 5-6. Are the bells you hear ringing in
   the fifth line the same as those you hear in the sixth ?
5. How shall we read the poem ?

Notes : page 90.

THE MINSTREL AT THE GATE

" Rokeby ", from which the following stanzas are taken, is a long poem telling a story of the Civil War.

It was a summer evening in the year 1644. A few days previously the battle of Marston Moor had overthrown the power of King Charles I in the North of England, and wrecked the fortunes of many of his friends. The Lord of Rokeby was a prisoner in the hands of Parliament, and Matilda, his daughter, had decided to abandon the home of her ancestors and seek safety elsewhere. With all in readiness for her departure at midnight, she was spending her last hours in Rokeby with a few companions before a wood fire in the hall.

While thus in peaceful guise they sate
A knock alarmed the outer gate,
And ere the tardy porter stirred
The tinkling of a harp was heard.
A manly voice, of mellow swell,   5
Bore burden to the music well.

" Summer eve is gone and past,
Summer dew is falling fast ;
I have wandered all the day,
Do not bid me farther stray !   10
Gentle hearts, of gentle kin,
Take the wandering harper in ! "

But the stern porter answer gave,
With " Get thee hence, thou strolling knave !
The king wants soldiers ; war, I trow,   15
Were meeter trade for such as thou."
At this unkind reproof, again
Answered the ready minstrel's strain.

" Bid not me, in battle-field,
Buckler lift, or broadsword wield !   20
All my strength and all my art
Is to touch the gentle heart
With the wizard notes that ring
From the peaceful minstrel-string."

The porter, all unmoved, replied,   25
" Depart in peace, with Heaven to guide ;
If longer by the gate thou dwell,
Trust me, thou shalt not part so well."   . . .

" I have song of war for knight,
Lay of love for lady bright,   30
Fairy tale to lull the heir,
Goblin grim the maids to scare ;
Dark the night, and long till day,
Do not bid me farther stray !

" Rokeby's lords of martial fame,   35
I can count them, name by name ;
Legends of their line there be,
Known to few, but known to me ;
If you honour Rokeby's kin
Take the wandering harper in.   40

" Rokeby's lords had fair regard
For the harp and for the bard ;
Baron's race throve never well
Where the curse of minstrel fell ;
If you love that noble kin,   45
Take the weary harper in ! "

SCOTT
(1771-1832)

18

The great days of the wandering minstrels were the 13th, 14th and 15th centuries. They had been the poets, the story-tellers, and the historians of the people, and had been welcomed everywhere by gentles and commons, for, in times when very few people could read, their songs and tales, recited to a harp accompaniment, had provided the entertainment that is now supplied by books. By the time of the Civil War such singers were held in little esteem. In another poem, " The Lay of the Last Minstrel ", Sir Walter Scott makes an aged harper, the sole survivor of them all, tell his final tale to the Duchess of Buccleuch about the end of the 17th century.

1. What forms of entertainment is this minstrel ready to offer ?

2. In which of his songs and tales is he likely to be most successful ?

3. Why does he speak of his *wizard* notes (line 23) ?

4. Why does the porter refuse him admittance ?

5. Write out (*a*) lines 7-12 ; (*b*) lines 15-16 and 26-28.

   Read them aloud and put this mark, /, above each syllable on which your voice lays stress.

   Which speech, the minstrel's or the porter's, runs with the gentler rhythm ?

6. In reading the poem it would be well to employ three people—the narrator (lines 1-6, 13, 17-18, 25), the minstrel (lines 7-12, 19-24, 29-46), the porter (lines 14-16, 26-28).

   What further suggestions can you make that will help to produce a lively and interesting rendering ?

   Notes : page 91.

THE TOY BAND

A Song of the Great Retreat   (1914-1918)

In the early days of the European War, German troops marched in great strength through Belgium towards the French frontier. A small British army sent forward to stay their progress was met at Mons by vastly superior numbers and forced to retreat. The enemy were relentless in pursuit, hoping if possible to destroy the entire force opposed to them, but the courage and endurance of the British soldiers proved equal to the strain.

Below you will read, both in verse and prose, how soldiers, beaten to the ground through sheer exhaustion, were pulled to their feet by the music of a tin whistle and a toy drum and led to safety out of " a very tight corner ". You may find it interesting to compare the ways in which poet and prose writer tell the same story.

Dreary lay the long road, dreary lay the town,
   Lights out and never a glint o' moon :
Weary lay the stragglers, half a thousand down,
   Sad sighed the weary big Dragoon.
" Oh ! if I'd a drum here to make them take the road
    again,   5
   Oh ! if I'd a fife to wheedle—come, boys, come !
You that mean to fight it out, wake and take your load
    again ;
   Fall in ! Fall in ! Follow the fife and drum !

" Hey, but here's a toy shop, here's a drum for me,
   Penny whistles too to play the tune !   10
Half a thousand dead men soon shall hear and see
   We're a band ! " said the weary big Dragoon.
" Rubadub ! Rubadub ! Wake and take the road again,
   Wheedle-deedle-deedle-dee, come, boys, come !
You that mean to fight it out, wake and take your load
    again,   15
   Fall in ! Fall in ! Follow the fife and drum ! "

Cheerly goes the dark road, cheerly goes the night,
   Cheerly goes the blood to keep the beat :

Half a thousand dead men marching on to fight
  With a little penny drum to lift their feet.   20
" Rubadub ! Rubadub ! Wake and take the road again,
  Wheedle-deedle-deedle-dee, come, boys, come !
You that mean to fight it out, wake and take your load
    again,
  Fall in ! Fall in ! Follow the fife and drum ! "

As long as there's an Englishman to ask a tale of me,   25
  As long as I can tell the tale aright,
We'll not forget the penny whistle's wheedle-deedle-dee
  And the big Dragoon a-beating down the night,
" Rubadub ! Rubadub ! Wake and take the road again,
  Wheedle-deedle-deedle-dee, come, boys, come !   30
You that mean to fight it out, wake and take your load
    again,
  Fall in ! Fall in ! Follow the fife and drum ! "

SIR HENRY NEWBOLT
(1862-1938)

1. How could you guess from the poem the kind of tunes
   that were played by whistle and drum ?
2. Why has the poet given us almost the same lines in the
   second half of each stanza ?
3. How will you read the poem ?

Notes : page 92.

Now read the Big Dragoon's own story.

THE RETREAT FROM MONS

" . . . I now collected all the stragglers I could
find and for a time had a miscellaneous commando of
about a hundred and fifty horse, composed chiefly of
the 5th Lancers and 4th Dragoon Guards (two Irish
regiments) . . .   5

" Approaching St. Quentin, the situation of the
infantry became precarious. Marched literally off
their feet, they straggled into the town in a demoralised
condition. In the early afternoon our Brigadier had
called the officers together and said we were in a very
tight corner, but must fight it out and die like gentle-
men. He appointed me rear-guard commander with two
squadrons and two companies of French Territorial
infantry in support. My orders were to hold the
Germans off and retire through St. Quentin at 6 p.m.
(I was not actually clear of it until six hours later.) . . .
" Our interpreter officer, Harrison (4th Hussars)
went into St. Quentin to find out if the infantry were
clear, as, barring an occasional solitary lame duck,
they seemed to have ceased coming down the le
Cateau road, a part of which we could see. On his
return, he reported the place swarming with stragglers,
he could find no officers, and the men were going into
the houses and lying down to sleep. . . .
" We gradually fell back into the town, leaving two
troops and machine-guns to hold the bridge over the
river. There were two or three hundred men lying
about in the Place and the few officers with them,
try as they would, could not get a kick out of them. . . .
" The men in the square were . . . so jaded it
was pathetic to see them. If one only had a band, I
thought ! Why not ? There was a toy-shop handy
which provided my trumpeter and myself with a tin
whistle and a drum and we marched round and round
the fountain where the men were lying like the dead,
playing ' The British Grenadiers ' and ' Tipperary '
and beating the drum like mad. They sat up and
began to laugh and even cheer. I stopped playing and
made them a short exhortation and told them I was
going to take them back to their regiments. They

began to stand up and fall in, and eventually we moved
slowly off into the night to the music of our improvised
band, now reinforced with a couple of mouth organs.
When well clear of the town I tried to delegate my
functions to someone else, but the infantry would not
let me go. 'Don't leave us, Major,' they cried, 'or,
by God, we'll not get anywhere.'   So on we went,
and it was early morning before I got back to my
squadron."

45

Lieut.-Gen. Sir Tom Bridges, k.c.b., k.c.m.g., d.s.o., ll.d.

(1871-1939)

From Alarms and Excursions

1. What do (*a*) " The Retreat From Mons ", (*b*) " The Toy
   Band " tell us regarding

    the scene,

    the time,

    the condition of the troops,

    the method by which they were brought back to action ?

    Arrange your answers in two columns, headed Prose and
   Poem.

2. What information does the prose supply that is omitted
   in the poem ?

3. Why does the poem not tell us the name of the town, the
   exact time, and the names of the tunes that were played ?

4. Suggest a title for each stanza of the poem, either a phrase
   from the stanza, or a word of your own.

5. To which stanza of the poem is there nothing in the prose
   to correspond ?   Why has the poet added it ?

Notes :   page 93.

THE KNIGHT'S LEAP

A Legend of Altenahr

" So the foemen have fired the gate, men of mine ;
  And the water is spent and gone ?
Then bring me a cup of the red Ahr-wine :
  I never shall drink but this one.

" And reach me my harness, and saddle my horse,   5
  And lead him me round to the door :
He must take such a leap to-night perforce
  As horse never took before.

" I have fought my fight, I have lived my life,
  I have drunk my share of wine :   10
From Trier to Cöln there was never a knight
  Lived a merrier life than mine.

" I have lived by the saddle for years twoscore ;
  And if I must die on tree,
Then the old saddle-tree, which has borne me of yore,   15
  Is the properest timber for me.

" So now to show bishop, and burgher, and priest
  How the Altenahr hawk can die :
If they smoke the old falcon out of his nest,
  He must take to his wings and fly."   20

He harnessed himself by the clear moonshine,
  And he mounted his horse at the door ;
And he drained such a cup of the red Ahr-wine
  As man never drained before.

He spurred the old horse, and he held him tight,   25
  And he leapt him out over the wall :
Out over the cliff, out into the night,
  Three hundred feet of fall.

They found him next morning below in the glen,
  With never a bone in him whole—   30
A mass or a prayer, now, good gentlemen,
  For such a bold rider's soul.

CHARLES KINGSLEY
(1819-1875)

24

Altenahr : *a town in Prussia on the Ahr, a tributary of the Rhine*
Trier : *Treves*   Cöln : *Cologne*   tree : *gallows tree*
saddle-tree : *wooden frame of the saddle*

1. Here is the story of the poem told in a paragraph of straight-
   forward prose :

   For forty years the citizens of Altenahr had been harried
   by a robber knight and his retainers. In vain they bought
   and sold and attempted to gather riches. Ever and again
   their enemies would swoop upon their merchandise and
   carry off the spoil to their castle on a rock so high that
   it seemed an impossibility to storm it. At long last, in
   a desperate attempt to free themselves from this
   oppression, the burghers besieged the castle with all the
   forces they could muster. Pressing ever and ever closer,
   they at length cut off the water supply of the besieged
   and succeeded one night in setting fire to the outer gate.
   Capture and the gallows were, it seemed, the robber
   knight's certain doom, but he had one way yet of escape.
   Donning his armour, and drinking a last huge cup of his
   favourite red wine, he mounted his warhorse and leapt
   him right over the castle wall into the glen, a sheer three
   hundred feet below. There next morning they found his
   broken body.

   (*a*) What differences do you note between the two
        ways of telling the story ?

   and (*b*) Why does the poem make us sympathise with the
        knight much more than the prose does ?

2. Which way of telling the story do you prefer ?
3. Describe the picture you would paint to illustrate the poem.
4. Here is a stanza such as might have been the first in the
   poem had it followed the ordinary prose order :

   Altenahr's burghers stored and planned,

   But in vain they planned and stored,

   For the knight of the crag and his robber band

   Swooped down on the burghers' hoard.

   Note the rhymes and the four-beat, three-beat rhythm of
   the lines.

   Now try to turn the following sentence into a second
   stanza. Omit words, add words, change words and the
   order of words as you please :

   They neither reaped corn nor pressed wine, but fell from
   the sky like hawks, until the burghers said, " We will
   harry their nest, for either the hawks must die, or we
   must ".

Notes : page 95.

LEEZIE LINDSAY

" Will you gang to the Highlands, Leezie Lindsay?
  Will you gang to the Highlands wi' me?
Will you gang to the Highlands, Leezie Lindsay,
  My bride and my darling to be? "

" To gang to the Highlands wi' you, sir,   5
  I dinna ken how that may be ;
For I ken na the land that you live in,
  Nor ken I the lad I'd gang wi'."

" O Leezie, lass, you maun ken little,
  If so be you dinna ken me ;   10
For my name is Lord Ronald Macdonald,
  A chieftain of high degree."

She has kilted her coats of green satin,
  She has kilted them up to the knee.
She's awa' wi' Lord Ronald Macdonald,   15
  His bride and his darling to be.

ANONYMOUS

gang : *go*   kilted : *tucked up*
wi' : *with*   coats : *skirts*
dinna ken : *do not know*   awa' : *away*
maun : *must*

ALLEN-A-DALE

Allen-a-Dale has no fagot for burning,
Allen-a-Dale has no furrow for turning,
Allen-a-Dale has no fleece for the spinning,
Yet Allen-a-Dale has red gold for the winning.
Come, read me my riddle ! come, hearken my tale !   5
And tell me the craft of bold Allen-a-Dale.

The Baron of Ravensworth prances in pride,
And he views his domains upon Arkindale side,
The mere for his net, and the land for his game,
The chase for the wild, and the park for the tame, 10
Yet the fish of the lake and the deer of the vale
Are less free to Lord Dacre than Allen-a-Dale !

Allen-a-Dale was ne'er belted a knight,
Though his spur be as sharp, and his blade be as bright ;
Allen-a-Dale is no baron or lord,   15
Yet twenty tall yeomen will draw at his word ;
And the best of our nobles his bonnet will vail,
Who at Rere-cross on Stanmore meets Allen-a-Dale.

Allen-a-Dale to his wooing is come ;
The mother, she ask'd of his household and home :   20
" Though the castle of Richmond stand fair on the hill,
My hall," quoth bold Allen, "shows gallanter still ;
'Tis the blue vault of heaven, with its crescent so pale,
And with all its bright spangles ! " said Allen-a-Dale.

The father was steel, and the mother was stone ;   25
They lifted the latch, and they bade him be gone ;
But loud, on the morrow, their wail and their cry ;
He had laugh'd on the lass with his bonny black eye,
And she fled to the forest to hear a love-tale,
And the youth it was told by was Allen-a-Dale !   30

SCOTT
(1771-1832)

1.   " *Will you gang to the pictures, Leezie Lindsay ?*
          Will you gang to the pictures wi' me ?
          Will you gang to the pictures, Leezie Lindsay,
           And then to the baker's for tea ? "
     Which is the better poetry, this, or stanza 1 of the poem ?

2. " Tell me the craft of bold Allen-a-Dale."

3. The daughter of a rich noble runs away from her home
     to wed Allen-a-Dale, a landless and houseless man.
     Why, as we read the poem, have we no sympathy for her
     father and mother ?

4. How far had you gone in your reading of " Allen-a-Dale "
     before you knew it was a cheerful, spirited poem ?

5. Compare Leezie Lindsay with the lass who fled to Allen-a-
     Dale.

6. Which of those poems takes us farther " off the ground " ?

Notes : page 96.

MY LADY GREENSLEEVES

Alas, my Love ! you do me wrong
    To cast me off discourteously ;
And I have loved you so long,
    Delighting in your company.

        Greensleeves was all my joy !
        Greensleeves was my delight !
        Greensleeves was my heart of gold ;
        And who but Lady Greensleeves ?

I have been ready at your hand,
    To grant whatever you would crave.
I have both waged life and land
    Your love and good will for to have.

I bought thee Petticoats of the best,
    The cloth so fine as fine might be !
I gave thee jewels for thy chest ;
    And all this cost I spent on thee !

Thy Girdle of gold so red,
    With pearls bedecked sumptuously :
The like no other lasses had ;
    And yet thou wouldst not love me !

Thy crimson Stockings, all of silk,
    With gold all wrought above the knee ;
Thy Pumps as white as was the milk ;
    And yet thou wouldst not love me !

Thy Gown was of the grassy green,
    Thy Sleeves of satin hanging by ;
Which made thee be our Harvest Queen :
    And yet thou wouldst not love me !

My gayest Gelding I thee gave,
    To ride wherever liked thee.
No lady ever was so brave :
    And yet thou wouldst not love me !

My Men were clothed all in green,
  And they did ever wait on thee;
All this was gallant to be seen: 35
  And yet thou wouldst not love me!

They set thee up, they took thee down;
  They served thee with humility:
Thy foot might not once touch the ground;
  And yet thou wouldst not love me!   40

Thou couldst desire no earthly thing,
  But still thou hadst it readily;
Thy Music still to play and sing;
  And yet thou wouldst not love me!

Greensleeves, now farewell! adieu!   45
  God I pray to prosper thee!
For I am still thy Lover true.
  Come once again and love me!

ANONYMOUS

waged : *pledged, hazarded*   gelding : *horse*
petticoats : *skirts*   brave : *fine, gay*
pumps : *shoes*

Lines 5-8 are the chorus, to be repeated after each stanza.

1. Describe the picture you would paint of Greensleeves.

2. This was a favourite song at the time of Queen Elizabeth. What makes us like it to-day?

3. Mark the " beats ", or stressed syllables, in lines 1-4 of this poem, and in lines 1-4 of " Allen-a-Dale ". You will find that there are four to the line in both stanzas.

Why are the poems so unlike in rhythm?

Notes : page 98.

THE WEE WEE MAN

As I was walking all alone,
  Between a water and a wa',
'Twas there I spied a wee wee man,
  And he was the least I ever saw.

His legs were scarce a shathmont's length,   5
  But thick and thimber was his thigh;
Between his brows there was a span,
  And between his shoulders there were three.

He took up a mickle stane,
  And he flung it far as I could see.   10
Though I had been a Wallace wight,
  I could not lift it to my knee.

" O wee wee man, but thou art strong!
  Oh, tell me where thy dwelling be."
" My dwelling's down by yon bonny bower,   15
  Oh, will you go with me and see? "

On we leapt, and away we rode,
  Till we came to the bonny green.
We lighted down to rest our horse,
  And out there came a lady sheen;   20

Four-and-twenty at her back,
  And they were all attired in green.
Though the King of Scotland had been there,
  The worst of them might have been his queen.

On we leapt, and away we rode,   25
  Till we came to the bonny hall
Where the roof was o' the beaten gold,
  And the floor was o' the crystal all.

When we came to the broad, broad stair,
  Ladies were dancing, jimp and sma';
But in the twinkling of an eye
  My wee wee man was clean awa'.

ANONYMOUS

wa' : *wall*
shathmont : *six inches*
thimber : *heavy*
span : *from thumb to little finger of outstretched hand*
mickle : *great*

Wallace wight : *strong as Wallace*
bower : *shady place*
sheen : *bright*
jimp : *neat, slender*
clean awa' : *quite gone*

This is a ballad, such as might have been told by the minstrel who came to Rokeby Hall. See pages 17-19, and note 1, page 91.

1. Describe the three pictures you see in the poem. Which colours would you use in painting them?

2. Is this a true story, or a fairy tale?

3. Would you have liked the poet to explain that this was an imaginary story—for example in an introductory stanza such as this:

> *Last night when all the house was still,*
> *Between the midnight and the day,*
> *'Twas then I dreamed a wondrous dream,*
> *As sleeping in my bed I lay?*

4. Which is your favourite stanza?

5. Which line gives us a hint of the pace at which we should read the poem?

Notes : page 99.

PUK-WUDJIES

They live 'neath the curtain
  Of fir woods and heather,
And never take hurt in
  The wildest of weather,
But best they love Autumn—she's brown as themselves—   5
And they are the brownest of all the brown elves ;
    When loud sings the West Wind,
    The bravest and best wind,
And puddles are shining in all the cart ruts,
    They turn up the dead leaves,   10
    The russet and red leaves,
Where squirrels have taught them to look out for nuts.

The hedge-cutters hear them
  Where berries are glowing,
The scythe circles near them   15
  At time of the mowing,
But most they love woodlands when Autumn's winds
    pipe,
And all through the cover the beechnuts are ripe,
    And great spikey chestnuts,
    The biggest and best nuts,   20
Blown down in the ditches, fair windfalls lie cast,
    And no tree begrudges
    The little Puk-Wudjies
A pocket of acorns, a handful of mast !

So should you be roaming   25
  Where branches are sighing,
When up in the gloaming
  The moon-wrack is flying,
And hear through the darkness, again and again,
'What's neither the wind nor the spatter of rain—   30
    A flutter, a flurry,
    A scuffle, a scurry,

A bump like the rabbits' that bump on the ground,
   A patter, a bustle
   Of small things that rustle,
You'll know the Puk-Wudjies are somewhere around !

PATRICK CHALMERS
(*20th Century*)

windfalls : *nuts blown down by the wind*
mast : *fruit of forest trees, such as acorns*
moon-wrack : *tattered clouds lit by the moon*

1. Are we more likely to see or to hear the Puk-Wudjies ?

2. Which lines tell us of the sounds they make ?

3. Find other " bumpy " or " rustly " lines in the poem.

4. Do the Puk-Wudjies walk and run as we do ?

5. Has the poem a walking, a running, or a " Puk-Wudjie " rhythm ?

6. Why do the Puk-Wudjies love Autumn best ? Give as many answers as you can.

7. Another poet, Longfellow, spoke of the " mischievous Puk-Wudjies ". Are our Puk-Wudjies mischievous ?

8. How shall we read the poem ?

Notes : page 100.

33

GRIM

Beside the blaze of forty fires
  Giant Grim doth sit,
Roasting a thick-wooled mountain sheep
  Upon an iron spit.
Above him wheels the winter sky,   5
  Beneath him, fathoms deep,
Lies hidden in the valley mists
  A village fast asleep—
Save for one restive hungry dog
  That, snuffing towards the height,   10
Smells Grim's broiled supper-meat, and spies
  His watch-fire twinkling bright.

WALTER DE LA MARE
(20*th* Century)

THE HORSEMAN

I heard a horseman
  Ride over the hill;
The moon shone clear,
  The night was still;
His helm was silver,   5
  And pale was he;
And the horse he rode
  Was of ivory.

WALTER DE LA MARE
(20*th* Century)

Here are two picture poems. Study them until you see each picture clearly.

1. Which picture is the bigger?
2. Which is the more easy to paint?
3. Which is the more still?
4. Which has the greater power of taking us " far away "?

Notes : page 102.

THREE CHARMS

I

In the morning when ye rise
Wash your hands and cleanse your eyes;
Next, be sure ye have a care
To disperse the water far;
For as far as it doth light,
So far keeps the evil sprite.

II

If ye will with Mab find grace,
Set each platter in his place;
Rake the fire up, and get
Water in ere sun be set.
Wash your pails, and cleanse your dairies:
Sluts are loathsome to the fairies.
Sweep your house—who doth not so,
Mab will pinch her by the toe.

III

If ye fear to be affrighted
When ye are by chance benighted,
In your pocket for a trust,
Carry nothing but a crust;
For that holy piece of bread
Charms the danger and the dread.

HERRICK
(1591-1674)

The word " charm " comes from a Latin word *carmen* meaning " a song ". Charms are little verses, or single lines, or even single words, that are supposed to have magic in them against the powers of evil. Long ago there were charms to cure toothache and fevers and squinting, for such misfortunes were supposed to be the work of evil spirits. To-day some people still seem to believe in charms, lucky words and lucky symbols—horseshoes, wishbones, and the like. But three hundred years ago, when Herrick wrote, such beliefs were much stronger and his poems would be read seriously by everyone.

1. Where should those charms be spoken?
2. Who should speak them, and in what voice should they be spoken?
3. Which charm seems to you the most magical?

Notes: page 102.

GALLOPING DICK

One hundred and twenty years ago,
   Over the heath-clad height,
Galloping Dick, the highwayman,
   Came riding through the night.
While down where the high road straggles   5
   'Twixt Oxford and Wycombe vale
The coachmen cursed, and his lordship cursed,
   And my lady's cheek was pale.
" But what care I ? " sang Galloping Dick,
   His pocket heavy with gems,   10
As his grey mare swung him up to the woods
   Above the glittering Thames.
Ah, never a gentleman of the road
   So brave and suave and quick
As the rogue they hanged at Aylesbury—   15
   Galloping Dick !

One hundred and twenty years ago,
   Across the heath-clad height,
Galloping Dick, the highwayman,
   Went riding through the night.   20
Now quiet homesteads cluster
   On the ridge near Wycombe town,
And farmers plough where the brambles grew,
   And they've hacked the forest down ;
And lovers stroll in the stony lane   25
   That dips to the highway still,
But never a highwayman flies past
   To hide on the lawless hill. . . .
For one hundred and twenty years ago
   When trees on the hill were thick,   30
They hanged the last of the highwaymen—
   Galloping Dick.

They hanged the last of the highwaymen—
  Yet when the night winds sigh
You'll hear the sound of clattering hoofs
  And a horseman gallops by.

ALMEY ST. JOHN ADCOCK
(*20th Century*)

1. The poem is written in three " chapters ", lines 1-16, 17-32, 33-36. Suggest a suitable title for each.
2. Lines 13-16. Suppose that instead of these lines the poet had written :

   > *Ah, never a gentleman of the road*
   >   *So brave and suave and quick*
   > *As the rider by night on the bonny grey mare—*
   >   *Galloping Dick* !

   How would the second stanza have been changed for us ?
3. Lines 16, 32. Why is *Galloping Dick* better than a longer line, for example, *Daredevil Galloping Dick* ?
4. Lines 1-4. Compare the first four lines of the poem with this version :

   > *More than a hundred and twenty years ago,*
   >   *Spurring his horse over the heath-clad height,*
   > *Galloping Dick, the reckless knight of the road,*
   >   *Time and again came riding hard through the night.*

   Which version do you prefer ?
5. What meaning do you give to " straggles " (line 5) " glittering " (line 12) " lawless " (line 28) ?
6. Galloping Dick was a rogue (line 15). Why do we like to read of him in this poem ?
7. How shall we read the poem ?

Notes : page 103.

THE FOX-CUB

" What is the sound, little brother,
  That rings thro' the early air ? "
" Oh, that is the call of the farmer-lads
  As the last of the sheaves they bear,
And they sing 'mid the dewy golden grain   5
  And laugh and make merry there."
But the old fox said : " That's the huntsman's call,
  Take care ! "

" What is the gleam, little brother,
  Showing white in the meadow there ? "   10
" Oh, the children gather the bramble fruit,
  And fill the pails they bear,
And they dance, white-clad, 'mong the crimsoning leaves,
  Or the purple beauty share."
But the old fox said : " That's the glint of hounds, 15
  Beware ! "

" What is the rustle, brother,
  That creeps through the covert there ? "
" Oh, the scent-soaked early morning breeze,
  Is stirring the bracken where   20
The green turns bronze—— Quick ! little brother,
  We'd best get back to our lair ! "
And the old fox he said nothing, for he
  Wasn't there.

HYLDA C. COLE
(*20th Century*)

1. Who are the speakers in the poem ?
2. Is this a true story ?
3. Is it funny or sad ?
4. We are to laugh at the " poetical " fox-cub. Are we,
   therefore, to laugh at poetry ?
5. How should each fox speak ?
6. Why is the poem called " The Fox-cub ", and not " The
   Old Fox " ?

Notes : page 104.

THE TORTOISESHELL CAT

The tortoiseshell cat
She sits on the mat,
As gay as a sunflower she;
In orange and black you see her blink,
And her waistcoat's white and her nose is p nk,
And her eyes are green as the sea.
But all is vanity, all the way;
Twilight's coming, and close of day,
And every cat in the twilight's gray,
Every possible cat.

The tortoiseshell cat
She is smooth and fat,
And we call her Josephine,
Because she weareth upon her back
This coat of colours, this raven black,
This red of the tangerine.
But all is vanity, all the way;
Twilight follows the brightest day,
And every cat in the twilight's gray,
Every possible cat.

PATRICK CHALMERS
(*20th Century*)

All is vanity: *All splendour passes away*
" All is vanity. All go unto one place; all
are of the dust, and all turn to dust again."
The Book of Ecclesiastes, iii, 19-20.

1. Why does the poet compare the cat to a sunflower?
2. Why do they call her Josephine?
3. Make a word-picture of her.
4. Do lines 17-20 merely repeat lines 7-10, or do they convey
   something more?
5. " All is vanity ". Is this a solemn poem?
6. How shall we say it?

Now you should read " On a Cat, Ageing ", page 40.

Notes: page 105.

ON A CAT, AGEING

He blinks upon the hearth-rug
And yawns in deep content,
Accepting all the comforts
That Providence has sent.

Louder he purrs, and louder,   5
In one glad hymn of praise
For all the night's adventures,
For quiet, restful days.

Life will go on for ever,
With all that cat can wish :   10
Warmth and the glad procession
Of fish and milk and fish.

Only—the thought disturbs him—
He's noticed once or twice,
The times are somehow breeding   15
A nimbler race of mice.

ALEXANDER GRAY
(*20th Century*)

1. In what ways does this cat resemble Josephine (page 39) ?
2. Which do you see more clearly ?
3. In which are you more interested ?
4. For lines 15-16 read the following :
       He cannot pounce so quickly
       As once he did, on mice.
   What have we lost ?
5. Does this poet hint that " All is vanity " ?
6. Which poem is the more amusing ?
7. Compare the rhythm of this poem with that of " The Tortoiseshell Cat ".

   Notes : page 106.

OLD WINTER

Old Winter sad, in snow yclad,
  Is making a doleful din ;
But let him howl till he crack his jowl,
  We will not let him in.

Ay, let him lift from the billowy drift   5
  His hoary, hagged form,
And scowling stand, with his wrinkled hand
  Outstretching to the storm.

Let his baleful breath shed blight and death
  On herb, and flower, and tree ;   10
And brooks and ponds in crystal bonds
  Bind fast ; but what care we ?

Let him push at the door, in the chimney roar,
  And rattle the window pane ;
Let him in at us spy with his icicle eye,   15
  But he shall not entrance gain.

Let him gnaw, forsooth, with his freezing tooth,
  On our roof tiles, till he tire ;
But we care not a whit as we jovial sit
  Before our blazing fire.   20

Come, lads, let's sing till the rafters ring ;
  Come, push the can about :
From our snug fire-side this Christmas-tide
  We'll keep Old Winter out.

THOMAS NOEL
(1799-1861)

yclad : *clad*   jowl : *jaw*   hagged : *haggard, or haglike*

1. In which stanza do you find the best picture of Old Winter ?
    Describe him as you see him there.
2. What do the other stanzas add to the picture ?
3. Choose lines that have a wintry sound.
4. Mark the rhyming words in stanza 1.   In how many of the
    other stanzas do you find rhyming words similarly placed ?
5. Make a stanza for yourself after the pattern of the second,
    the third, or the fifth.
6. Which line or lines tell you most clearly how to say the
    poem ?

Notes : page 106.

EDDI'S SERVICE

Eddi, priest of St. Wilfrid
    In the chapel at Manhood End,
Ordered a midnight service
    For such as cared to attend.

But the Saxons were keeping Christmas,   5
    And the night was stormy as well.
Nobody came to service
    Though Eddi range the bell.

" Wicked weather for walking,"
    Said Eddi of Manhood End.   10
" But I must go on with the service
    For such as care to attend."

The altar-candles were lighted—
    An old marsh donkey came,
Bold as a guest invited,   15
    And stared at the guttering flame.

The storm beat on at the windows,
    The water splashed on the floor,
And a wet, yoke-weary bullock
    Pushed in through the open door,   20

" How do I know what is greatest,
    How do I know what is least?
That is My Father's business,"
    Said Eddi, Wilfrid's priest.

" But—three are gathered together—   25
    Listen to me and attend.
I bring good news, my brethren ! "
    Said Eddi of Manhood End.

And he told the Ox of a Manger
  And a Stall in Bethlehem,
And he spoke to the Ass of a Rider,
  That rode to Jerusalem.

They steamed and dripped in the chancel,
  They listened and never stirred,
While, just as though they were Bishops,
  Eddi preached them The Word.

Till the gale blew off on the marshes
  And the windows showed the day,
And the Ox and the Ass together
  Wheeled and clattered away.

And when the Saxons mocked him,
  Said Eddi of Manhood End,
" I dare not shut His chapel
  On such as care to attend."

RUDYARD KIPLING
(1865-1936)

St. Wilfrid lived in the seventh century. Most of his days were spent in Yorkshire, but at one time, while seeking refuge from King Ecgfrid, he worked among the Saxons of Sussex. Eddius, or Eddi, was his devoted friend and follower.

This poem comes from " Rewards and Fairies ", a book in which we read how Puck shows two present-day Sussex children scenes from the past history of the country-side they know. There you will learn how Eddi first came to respect animals.

1. Why did Eddi tell the Ox of a Manger, and the Ass of a Rider that rode to Jerusalem ?

2. In which stanza do you find the most striking picture ?

3. Show from the poem that Eddi was simple of heart, and a true follower of Christ.

4. Show that the poet was right to tell his story in a simple way.

Notes : page 108.

A CHRISTMAS CAROL

In the bleak mid-winter
  Frosty wind made moan,
Earth stood hard as iron,
  Water like a stone ;
Snow had fallen, snow on snow,   5
  Snow on snow,
In the bleak mid-winter
  Long ago.

Our God, Heaven cannot hold Him,
  Nor earth sustain ;   10
Heaven and earth shall flee away
  When He comes to reign :
In the bleak mid-winter
  A stable-place sufficed
The Lord God Almighty   15
  Jesus Christ. . . .

CHRISTINA ROSSETTI
(1830-1894)

1. Are there any difficult words in stanza 1 ?
2. Line 3. What meaning do you give to " stood " ?
3. Lines 5 and 6. Compare these lines with

> *Everything was buried*
> *Under snow.*

   Which do you prefer ?
4. Which word in stanza 1 best describes the picture the poet
   has put before us ?
5. The first stanza gives us a picture. The second stanza
   gives us something to think about. Put the thought
   very simply in your own words.
6. Would stanza 2 have meant as much to us if we had not
   first read stanza 1 ?
7. At what speed shall we read this poem ?

Notes : page 108.

THE FROZEN OCEAN

The sea would flow no longer,
  It wearied after change,
It called its tides and breakers in,
  From where they might range.

It sent an icy message   5
  To every wave and rill;
They lagged, they paused, they stiffened,
  They froze, and were still.

It summoned in its currents,
  They reached not where they led;   10
It bound its foaming whirl-pools.
  " Not the old life," it said,

" Not fishes for the fishermen,
  Not bold ships as before,
Not beating loud for ever   15
  Upon the seashore,

" But cold white foxes stepping
  On to my hard proud breast,
And a bird coming sweetly
  And building a nest.   20

" My icebergs shall be mountains,
  My silent fields of snow
Unmarked shall join the lands' snowfields—
  Where,   no man shall know."

VIOLA MEYNELL
(20th Century)

1. Make from the poem two pictures, one of " the old life "
   (line 12) the other of the new life the sea wearied after.
2. Contrast the picture in " A Christmas Carol ", lines 1-8,
   and the picture in lines 17-24 of this poem.
3. Read again stanzas 2, 3 and 6. Why is it that we must
   take each slowly ?

   Notes : page 109.

45

THE LITTLE YOUNG LAMBS

             In the fold
             On the wold
         There were little young lambs,
             An' the wind blew so cold
         They laid lee' o' their dams,   5
             An' a shepherd old man
         He leaned over the cotes,
             An' a lilt be began
         With a flutter of notes,
     The little young lambs all among ;   10
 Oh, he piped 'em a derry down derry, he did,
             Since they were so young.

             An' they stirred
             When they heard,
         Did the little young lambs,   15
             Then they hopped, most absurd,
         From a-lee of their dams,
             An' they jumped and they skipped
         With tip-toppetty skips,
             As the little tune tripped   20
         From the reed at the lips
     Of the crinkled old man o' the wold,
 As he piped 'em a derry down derry, he did,
             Since he was so old.

             For he blew   25
             That he knew
         Why the seasons went round,
             An' why green the wheat grew
         To his pipe's pretty sound ;
             An' why rain follows sun,   30

An' how sun follows rain,
  An' how everything's done
To be started again,
Till the stars like ripe acorns shall fall ;
An' he piped 'em his derry down derry, he did.   35
  Along of it all.

PATRICK R. CHALMERS
(20*th* Century)

lee o' their dams : *on the lee, or sheltered, side of their mothers*
cotes : *enclosures, shelters*

1. Describe the old man you would draw to illustrate this poem.
2. What kind of tune did he play ?
3. Was it a good tune for lambs to skip to ?
4. Was it a magic tune like that of " The Fiddle " (page 14) ?
5. Is this a winter, or a spring, poem ?
6. How shall we read it ?

Notes : page 110.

A BIT OF COLOUR

Gray was the morn, all things were gray,
  'Twas winter more than spring;
A bleak east wind swept o'er the land,
  And sobered everything.

Gray was the sky, the fields were gray,
  The hills, the woods, the trees—
Distance and foreground—all the scene
  Was gray in the gray breeze.

Gray cushions, and a gray skin rug,
  A dark gray wicker trap,
Gray were the ladies' hats and cloaks,
  And gray my coat and cap;

A narrow, lonely, gray, old lane;
  And lo, on a gray gate,
Just by the side of a gray wood,
  A sooty sweep there sat!

With grimy chin 'twixt grimy hands
  He sat and whistled shrill;
And in his sooty cap he wore
  A yellow daffodil.

And often, when the days are dull,
  I seem to see him still—
The jaunty air, the sooty face,
  And the yellow daffodil.

HORACE SMITH
(19*th Century*)

distance and foreground: *the far-off scene and the scene close
  to the eyes*
trap: *pony-carriage*

1. Which colour has the poet used most freely?
2. Which colour stands out most clearly in the finished
  picture?
3. Line 22. Why does the poet " seem to see him still "?

Notes: page 111.

WHAT THE WEATHER DOES

The rooks are alive
  On the tops of the trees;
They look like a hive
  Of jolly black bees;
They all squawk together,   5
  And loud is their squawking—
It must be the weather
  That sets them a-talking.

A lark in the sky
  Climbs up as it sings;   10
I watch it soar high
  And I wish I had wings;
The birds sing together
  With merry notes ringing—
It must be the weather   15
  That sets them a-singing.

The frost and the snow
  Have gone from the lane;
They both had to go
  When the sun came again;   20
They skulked off together,
  As out I came prancing,
It *must* be the weather
  That sets me a-dancing.

HAMISH HENDRY
(*20th Century*)

1. When did you learn that this was to be a cheerful poem?
2. Compare the day that this poem describes with that described in " A Bit of Colour ".
3. Which do you prefer, the first stanza of the poem or this shorter version:

> *The rooks stir in the tree-tops;*
>   *Like big black bees they swarm;*
> *All at once squawk loudly*
>   *Because the sun is warm?*

4. How shall we read the poem?
Notes: page 111.

THE BLACKBIRD

He comes on chosen evenings,
My blackbird bountiful, and sings
Over the gardens of the town
Just at the hour the sun goes down.
His flight across the chimneys thick,   5
By some divine arithmetic,
Comes to his customary stack,
And couches there his plumage black,
And there he lifts his yellow bill,
Kindled against the sunset, till   10
These suburbs are like Dymock woods
Where music has her solitudes,
And while he mocks the winter's wrong
Rapt on his pinnacle of song,
Figured above our garden plots   15
Those are celestial chimney-pots.

JOHN DRINKWATER
(1882-1937)

1. Where does this blackbird sing?

2. At what season does he sing?

3. Why does the poet call him " *my* blackbird *bountiful* "?

4. In which line does the poet best praise his song?

5. In the last five pages you have read four spring poems. If you were arranging them in pairs, which would you place beside " The Little Young Lambs ", and which beside " A Bit of Colour "?

Notes : page 112.

THE GLASS SHIP

I see it daily as I pass—
A tiny ship of sparkling glass
Within a delicate crystal case,
Riding the waves with shining grace ;
Spars, masts and rigging all complete,   5
Most exquisitely fine and neat.

The little shop is small and dim
And overflowing to the brim,
And in the dingy window space
A hundred huddled things find place :   10
Odd cups and saucers, pinch-beck rings,
A violin bereft of strings,
A gaunt, dejected feather fan,
Discoloured ivories from Japan,
A tattered shawl that once was gay,   15
Chessmen with pieces broken away,
Pale samplers, mildew-spotted prints
And crumpled piles of faded chintz.

But bright among this drab array
The little ship pursues its way   20
Upon some fairy mission bent—
Some secret far accomplishment.
And children stop and point and stare
To see a thing so frail and fair,
Then turn away with envious eyes   25
Where yet some dreaming hope may rise
Of finding in the puddled street
A tiny glittering crystal fleet.

Rose Fyleman
(20th Century)

(Reproduced by permission of the Proprietors of " Punch ".)

1. How does the little ship differ from the " drab array "
   of lines 7-18 ?
2. Is it good for the children to see the ship ?
3. Is this a good subject for a poem ?
4. Suggest similar subjects for " city " poems.

   Notes : page 112.

BLUE STARS AND GOLD

While walking through the trams and cars
I chanced to look up at the sky,
And saw that it was full of stars !

So starry-sown ! A man could not,
With any care, have stuck a pin   5
Through any single vacant spot.

And some were shining furiously ;
And some were big and some were small ;
But all were beautiful to see.

Blue stars and gold ! A sky of grey !   10
The air between a velvet pall !
I could not take my eyes away !

And there I sang this little psalm
Most awkwardly ! Because I was
Standing between a car and tram !   15

JAMES STEPHENS
(20th Century)

1. How many lines deal with trams and cars ; how many
   deal with the sky ?
2. Was it a still, or a windy night ?
3. Was the poet wise to look at the stars ?
4. " The Blackbird ", " The Glass Ship ", " Blue Stars and
   Gold " are all town poems.   Would you have discovered
   this from their titles ?
5. If you stay in a town, try to make a poem about some-
   thing you know. Here is an opening stanza on the same
   pattern as those in the poem you have just read :

   > *From my high window 'neath the stars*
   > *I looked down on the street below,*
   > *And saw the swift and shining cars.*

Notes : page 113.

COUNTRY BUSES

The stolid London buses roll down the cars between
And halt before the red lights and hurry past the green ;
Through crowded streets of traffic, from Chelsea to
    St. Paul's,
They make their careful journeys from dawn till
    evening falls.

But the happy country buses they are free to bowl   5
    along
Through little scattered hamlets where the names are
    like a song,
Where Blyth Bridge and Bonnybridge and Lilliesleaf
    and Luss
Hang out their lights on winter nights to greet the
    country bus.

By open fields and far-flung woods, o'er hills and vales
    they speed
To link us with the villages and serve our rustic need.   10
They wait for us at nameless gates and bridges and
    road-ends,
And all along the country miles the buses are our
    friends.

And when alone with stick and dog we tramp the roads
    and tire
The kind bus overtakes us and we pay the modest hire
And are whirled to home and firelight, sitting lordly   15
    at our ease,
With the country folk to talk to and the dog between
    our knees

The busy London buses with their hundred stops and
    starts
Take up a million passengers but never win their
    hearts ;
But the friendly country buses, as they run from town
    to town,
They know us when we board them and they know   20
    where we get down.

WILL H. OGILVIE
(20th Century)

(Reproduced by permission of the Proprietors of " Punch ".)

1. What are the four most important things you are told
   about the London buses in stanza 1, and about the
   country buses in stanza 2 ?

2. Can you tell from these two stanzas whether the writer
   was a countryman or a townsman ?

3. Can you prove your answer correct from stanzas 3-5 ?

4. Suppose the writer had been a townsman, how might he
   have spoken of the London buses and the country buses ?

5. Which do you prefer—the town buses or the country
   buses ?

6. Do the buses go fast ?

7. If you had written line 5 of this poem in your composition
   you would probably have omitted one word. Which ?

8. How does the writer regard the country buses ?

Notes : page 114.

54

FROM A RAILWAY CARRIAGE

Faster than fairies, faster than witches,
Bridges and houses, hedges and ditches ;
And charging along like troops in a battle,
All through the meadows the horses and cattle :
All of the sights of the hill and the plain   5
Fly as thick as driving rain ;
And ever again, in the wink of an eye,
Painted stations whistle by.

Here is a child who clambers and scrambles,
All by himself and gathering brambles ;   10
Here is a tramp who stands and gazes ;
And there is the green for stringing the daisies !
Here is a cart run away in the road
Lumping along with man and load ;
And here is a mill and there is a river :   15
Each a glimpse and gone for ever !

R. L. STEVENSON
(1850-1894)

1. Where is the speaker ?

2. What time of day is it ?

3. What season of the year is it ?

4. Do you see the train ?

5. Why are there so many pictures and why are they so short ?

6. Name all the things in the first stanza that

   Fly as thick as driving rain, faster than fairies, fast
   than witches.

7. How fast is this train going ?

8. What is the mood of the speaker ?

Notes : page 115.

THE TRAIN

A green eye—and a red—in the dark,
Thunder—smoke—and a spark.

It is there—it is here—flashed by,
Whither will the wild thing fly?

It is rushing, tearing thro' the night,   5
Rending her gloom in its flight.

It shatters her silence with shrieks,
What is it the wild thing seeks?

Alas! for it hurries away
Them that are fain to stay.   10

Hurrah! for it carries home
Lovers and friends that roam.

Where are you, Time and Space?
The world is a little place,

Your reign is over and done,   15
You are one.

MARY COLERIDGE
(1861-1907)

1. This train, like that in " From a Railway Carriage ", is
   an " express ". Why is it so different from the other?
2. Which line and which word in it make us feel most the
   speed of the train?
3. This poem divides naturally into three parts. What does
   each part do?
4. How fast is this train going?
5. In the last poem we could hear the beat, the rhythm of
   the train. Can you hear it in this one?
6. Suppose the last two lines had gone thus:

   > *Your reign is over and done*
   > *For you are really one.*

   Would that be as good?
7. How does this poet think of the train?

Notes: page 116.

BORDER MARCH

March, march, Ettrick, and Teviotdale,
  Why the deil dinna ye march forward in order?
March, march, Eskdale and Liddesdale,
  All the Blue Bonnets are bound for the Border.
    Many a banner spread
    Flutters above your head,
  Many a crest that is famous in story.
    Mount and make ready then,
    Sons of the mountain glen,
  Fight for the Queen and our old Scottish glory.

Come from the hills where your hirsels are grazing,
  Come from the glen of the buck and the roe;
Come to the crag where the beacon is blazing,
  Come with the buckler, the lance, and the bow.
    Trumpets are sounding,
    War-steeds are bounding,
  Stand to your arms, and march in good order;
    England shall many a day
    Tell of the bloody fray,
  When the Blue Bonnets came over the Border.

SCOTT
(1771-1832)

hirsels: *flocks*

1. In some of the poems in this book the chief interest has been
   the story, in others the pictures they brought to our
   minds. Here the poet has interested us chiefly in the
   sound of his stanzas. Was he right to do so?

2. In the first four lines how many things can you find that
   bring out the sound?

3. In some books lines 5-10 are printed thus:

   Many a banner spread flutters above your head,
   Many a crest that is famous in story.
   Mount and make ready then, sons of the mountain glen,
   Fight for the Queen and our old Scottish glory.

   Does this make any difference?

4. How does the speaker feel in this poem?

   Notes: page 117.

THE SONG OF THE WESTERN MEN

A good sword and a trusty hand !
  A merry heart and true !
King James's men shall understand
  What Cornish lads can do.

And have they fixed the where and when ?   5
  And shall Trelawny die ?
Then twenty thousand Cornish men
  Will know the reason why !

Out spake their captain brave and bold,
  A merry wight was he :   10
" If London Tower were Michael's Hold,
  We'll set Trelawny free !

" We'll cross the Tamar, land to land,
  The Severn is no stay,
With one and all, and hand in hand,   15
  And who shall bid us nay ?

" And when we come to London Wall,
  A pleasant sight to view,
Come forth ! come forth, ye cowards all,
  Here's men as good as you !   20

" Trelawny he's in keep and hold,
  Trelawny he may die ;
But here's twenty thousand Cornish bold,
  Will know the reason why ! "

HAWKER
(1803-1875)

King James : *James II*
Trelawny : *one of the Seven Bishops*
Michael's Hold : *St. Michael's Mount*
Tamar : *river forming boundary between Cornwall and Devon*
1. How does the speaker feel in this poem ?
2. There is a definite challenge in the poem. How often is
   it repeated ?
3. What is the difference between the feelings of the speaker
   in this poem and those of the speaker in the " Border
   March " ?
4. Why are we so entirely on the side of the Cornish lads,
   ready to march with them and fight for Trelawny ?

Notes : page 118.

SONG OF THE BROWN SEA RAT

Now we are the rodent mariners,
  As nobody needs be told,
For there's no mistaking our nautical airs,
  Our rolling eyes and bold ;
And 'tis never a ship leaves English ground
From Liverpool Docks to Plymouth Sound,
For San Francisco or Bombay bound,
  But we have the run of her hold.

With a pit-a-pit pat
  And a chip chip chip,
'Tis the brown sea rat
  That is captain of the ship !

We go aboard in companies,
  Marching at dead of night
Over the hawsers from the quays
  By starlight and lamplight :
Each roving rat his ship will choose,
From nose to nose we pass the news
Of cargoes, destinations, crews,
  And naught can us affright.

With a churr churr a-churr
  And a quee quee quee,
'Tis the rodent mariner
  That is lord of the sea !

Was ever king as sea rat rich?
   Each vessel leaving land
A wandering larder is, in which
   Lie feasts on every hand: 25
Maize, apples, salmon, barley, rice,
Nutmegs, beans, olives, South Sea spice, 30
Meats, cheeses, India merchandise,
   And all at our command!

With a ho ho ho
   And a ho once again,
Whatever winds may blow, 35
   We are masters of the main!

We know the ports of all the world,
   All warehouses, all quays,
All islets coral-ringed and pearled,
   The blue Hesperides: 40
And men may search until they die,
And men may blow great fleets sky-high—
But we alone can hold for aye
   The Freedom of the Seas!

With a pit-a-pit pat 45
   And a chip chip chip,
'Tis the brown sea rat
   That is captain of the ship.

With a churr churr a-churr
   And a quee quee quee, 50
'Tis the rodent mariner
   That is lord of the sea.

With a ho ho ho
  And a ho once again,
Whatever winds may blow,
  We are masters of the main !

55

HAMISH MACLAREN
(20th Century)

1. Generally we don't like rats, but we do like the Brown
   Sea Rat, he is such a jolly fellow and sings such a jolly
   song.

   Another name for this poem might have been " Song and
   Dance of the Brown Sea Rat ". Why ?

2. Surely stanza 3 is the finest feast you ever read of. In
   " The Pied Piper ", page 80, lines 127-145, you will find
   another rat's description of a feast. Which of the two
   would you prefer to share ?

3. Stanza 2 tells us how the rats pass from ship to ship. When
   all the rats leave a ship it is considered a very bad sign.

   Here is a passage from " Youth ", a story by Joseph Conrad.

   " Then, on a fine moonlight night, all the rats left the ship.
   " We had been infested with them. They had destroyed
   our sails, consumed more stores than the crew, affably shared
   our beds and our dangers, and now, when the ship was made
   seaworthy, concluded to clear out. I called Mahon to enjoy
   the spectacle. Rat after rat appeared on our rail, took a last
   look over his shoulder, and leaped with a hollow thud into the
   empty hulk. We tried to count them, but soon lost the tale.
   Mahon said : ' Well, well ! don't talk to me about the
   intelligence of rats. They ought to have left before, when we
   had that narrow squeak from foundering. There you have
   the proof how silly is the superstition about them. They
   leave a good ship for an old rotten hulk, where there is nothing
   to eat, too, the fools ! . . . I don't believe they know what
   is safe or what is good for them, any more than you or I ! '

   " And after some more talk we agreed that the wisdom of
   rats had been grossly overrated, being in fact no greater than
   that of men."

   [But the rats were right. The ship's cargo of coal was in
   bad condition, and afterwards took fire ; and the ship sank.]

   Notes : page 119.

61

SAM

When Sam goes back in memory,
  It is to where the sea
Breaks on the shingle, emerald-green,
  In white foam, endlessly ;
He says—with small brown eye on mine—
  " I used to keep awake,
And lean from my window in the moon,
  Watching those billows break.
And half a million tiny hands,
  And eyes, like sparks of frost,
Would dance and come tumbling into the moon
  On every breaker tossed.
And all across from star to star,
  I've seen the watery sea
With not a single ship in sight,
  Just ocean there, and me ;
And heard my father snore. And once,
  As sure as I'm alive,
Out of those wallowing, moon-flecked waves
  I saw a mermaid dive ;
Head and shoulders above the wave,
  Plain as I now see you,
Combing her hair, now back, now front,
  Her two eyes peeping through ;
Calling me, ' Sam ! '—quietlike—' Sam ! ' . .
  But me . . . I never went,
Making believe I kind of thought
  'Twas some one else she meant . . .

Wonderful lovely there she sat,
    Singing the night away,
All in the solitudinous sea
    Of that there lonely bay.   **30**

P'raps," and he'd smooth his hairless mouth,
    " P'raps, if 'twere now, my son,
P'raps, if I heard a voice say, ' Sam ! ' . . .   35
    Morning would find me gone."

WALTER DE LA MARE
(*20th Century*)

1. Is Sam a young man or an old man ?

2. Where has he spent his life ?

3. Where is he when he tells his story ?

4. How does he tell his story—slowly or quickly, quietly and earnestly, or is he just trying to amuse the little boy he calls " my son " ?

5. Line 17. " And heard my father snore ". Why do you think this is brought in ?

Notes : page 120.

THE LOWLANDS OF HOLLAND

" My love he's built a bonnie ship, and set her on the sea,
With seven score guid mariners to bear her companie.
There's three score is sunk, and three score dead at sea ;
And the Lowlands of Holland hae twined my love and me.

My love he built another ship, and set her on the main,   5
And nane but twenty mariners for to bring her hame ;
But the weary wind began to rise, and the sea began
    to route ;
My love then, and his bonnie ship turned withershins
    about.

There shall neither coif come on my head, nor comb
    come in my hair ;
There shall neither coal nor candle-light come in my
    bower mair ;   10
Nor will I love another man until the day I dee,
For I never loved a love but ane, and he's drowned in
    the sea."

" Oh haud your tongue, my daughter dear, be still and
    be content ;
There are mair lads in Galloway, ye need na sair
    lament."
" Oh ! there is nane in Galloway, there's nane at a'
    for me ;   15
For I never loved a love but ane, and he's drowned in
    the sea."
                              ANONYMOUS

twined : *parted*   withershins : *from right to left*
route : *roar*   coif : *girl's headdress*

1. The story of the poem is contained in the first two stanzas.
   In the first we are given the journey to Holland. What
   things are we not told about this journey that we should
   like to know ?

2. Stanza 2 gives the return journey. Are there any questions
   we should like to ask about it ?

3. Why does the lady tell the story in this way ?

4. In some versions this poem stops at line 12. Do you think
   the fourth stanza should be omitted ?

   Notes : page 121.

THE TARRY BUCCANEER

I'm going to be a pirate with a bright brass pivot-gun,
And an island in the Spanish Main beyond the setting sun,
And a silver flagon full of red wine to drink when work
    is done,
  Like a fine old salt-sea scavenger, like a tarry Buccaneer.

With a sandy creek to careen in, and a pig-tailed Spanish   5
    mate,
And under my main-hatches a sparkling merry freight
Of doubloons and double moidores and pieces of eight,
  Like a fine old salt-sea scavenger, like a tarry Buccaneer.

With a taste for Spanish wine-shops and for spending
    my doubloons,
And a crew of swart mulattoes and black-eyed octoroons,   10
And a thoughtful way with mutineers of making them
    maroons,
  Like a fine old salt-sea scavenger, like a tarry Buccaneer.

With a sash of crimson velvet and a diamond-hilted sword,
And a silver whistle about my neck secured to a golden cord,
And a habit of taking captives and walking them along   15
    a board,
  Like a fine old salt-sea scavenger, like a tarry Buccaneer.

With a spy-glass tucked beneath my arm and a cocked
    hat cocked askew,
And a long low rakish schooner a-cutting of the waves
    in two,
And a flag of skull and cross-bones the wickedest that
    ever flew,
  Like a fine old salt-sea scavenger, like a tarry Buccaneer.   20

JOHN MASEFIELD
(*20th Century*)

1. How old is the speaker in this poem, and what line in the
   poem tells you this most clearly?
2. Does he really wish to be a Tarry Buccaneer?
3. This poem does not tell you a story but makes you see
   pictures. Give a full picture of the " pirate " and his ship.
4. The speaker seems to be walking up and down like the
   captain on his quarterdeck. If you were walking and
   repeating the poem, how many steps would you take to
   each line?

Notes : page 122.

THE VAGABOND

I know the pools where the grayling rise,
  I know the trees where the filberts fall,
I know the woods where the red fox lies,
  The twisted elms where the brown owls call.
And I've seldom a shilling to call my own,   5
  And there's never a girl I'd marry.
I thank the Lord I'm a rolling stone
  With never a care to carry.

I talk to the stars as they come and go
  On every night from July to June,   10
I'm free of the speech of the winds that blow,
  And I know what weather will sing what tune.
I sow no seed and I pay no rent,
  And I thank no man for his bounties,
But I've a treasure that's never spent,   15
  I'm lord of a dozen counties.

JOHN DRINKWATER
(1882-1937)

1. Is the vagabond quite contented ?
2. Where is his home ?
3. In what sense is he " lord of a dozen counties " ?
4. Would you like to be the vagabond ?
5. Why ?
6. Compare the rhythm of this poem with that of " The Lowlands of Holland " (page 64).

Notes : page 122.

HIE AWAY

Hie away, hie away,
Over bank and over brae,
Where the copsewood is the greenest,
Where the fountains glisten sheenest,
Where the lady-fern grows strongest,   5
Where the morning dew lies longest,
Where the blackcock sweetest sips it,
Where the fairy latest trips it ;
Hie to haunts right seldom seen,
Lovely, lonesome, cool, and green,   10
Over bank and over brae,
Hie away, hie away !

Scott
(1771-1832)

1. What do you notice about lines 3-8 and about lines 11-12 ?

2. Which couplet (two lines) in this poem do you like best ?

3. Are the feelings of the speaker in this poem the same as
those of the Vagabond (page 66) ?

Notes :   page 123.

IN SUMMER TIME

In Summer time, when flowers do spring,
  And birds sit on each tree,
Let lords and knights say what they will,
  There's none so merry as we.
There's Will and Moll, with Harry and Doll,   5
  And Tom and bonny Bettee ;
Oh ! how they do whisk it, caper, and frisk it
  Under the greenwood tree.

Our music is a little pipe
  That can so sweetly play ;   10
We hire old Hal from Whitsuntide
  Till latter Lammas Day ;
In Summer morns and holidays,
  At even, too, comes he,
And then we do skip it, caper, and trip it,   15
  Under the greenwood tree. . .

ANONYMOUS

Whitsuntide : *late May or early June*
Lammas Day : *first day of August*

1. Who is the speaker in this poem ?

2. What is he telling us about ?

3. How does the manner in which he tells us help us to feel
  the joy and light-heartedness of it all ?

Notes : page 124.

CARGOES

Quinquireme of Nineveh from distant Ophir,
Rowing home to haven in sunny Palestine,
With a cargo of ivory,
And apes and peacocks,
Sandalwood, cedarwood, and sweet white wine.   5

Stately Spanish galleon coming from the Isthmus,
Dipping through the Tropics by the palm-green shores,
With a cargo of diamonds,
Emeralds, amethysts,
Topazes, and cinnamon, and gold moidores.   10

Dirty British coaster with a salt-caked smoke-stack,
Butting through the Channel in the mad March days,
With a cargo of Tyne coal,
Road-rails, pig-lead,
Firewood, iron-ware, and cheap tin trays.   15

JOHN MASEFIELD
(20th Century)

1. If you were asked to paint three pictures, one for each stanza in this poem, what would they be?

2. What would probably not appear at all in your pictures?

3. Why is the poem called " Cargoes "?

4. What kind of weather is it in your picture for the **first** stanza?

5. Some people think that Mr. Masefield is speaking with contempt of the " dirty British coaster ", or laughing at it? Do you?

6. To whom do you think the Quinquireme of Nineveh belonged?

Notes : page 124.

SOLOMON AND THE MONKEYS

Apes and peacocks and almug and ivory
  Solomon sent for over seas,
And, if you ask me the reason why for he
  Sent his shipping for such as these—
Peacocks flaunt like an opal necklace,   5
Figurey almug's fair and fleckless,
Ivory's smooth and white and speckless
  (Tusks on a plinth of gold)
And the little grey monkeys, so wrinkled wise,
Little grey apes with the twinkling eyes,   10
  Puckered, brown and cold,
'Spite of their lightsome ways and reckless,
Know the wisdom of gods of old !

Solomon sat by his garden palaces
  Seeking wisdom of earth and air ;   15
Little grey apes, full of mocks and malices,
  Chipped and chattered around his chair ;
Chipped and chattered and made grimaces,
Rubbed their backs and their wrinkled faces,
Swung themselves with a score of graces   20
  Through the cedar trees :
But never their knowledge could Solomon catch,
For, if he asked them, they'd only scratch,
  Stop and scratch for fleas ;
Then they'd rocket away in races,   25
Ruffling, scuffling in twos and threes !

So Solomon sent for Hiram, King o' Tyre—
  Hiram strode 'neath the budding leaf,
Purple vesture and golden ring, attire
  Fit indeed for a merchant chief—   30
He bade him watch the monkeys slipping
Through the pomegranate branches dipping
Over the fountains ferned and dripping,
  Green and clear and cold ;

And " 'Tis excellent knowledge," King Hiram said,   35
" That keeps its learning inside its head ;
   That's your monkey's gold—
That's the reason that sets them skipping—
That's their wisdom of gods of old ! "

PATRICK CHALMERS
(20*th Century*)

almug : *a kind of timber*   plinth : *base*

1. Of what does the first line remind you ?

2. The poem has a humorous side to it. How far do you
read before you realise this ?

3. Did Solomon think the apes were wise ?

4. Why did he send for Hiram ?

5. Did Hiram think the apes were wise ?

Notes : page 126.

ROAD-SONG OF THE *BANDAR-LOG*

Here we go in a flung festoon,
Half-way up to the jealous moon!
Don't you envy our pranceful bands?
Don't you wish you had extra hands?
Wouldn't you like if your tails were—*so*—   5
Curved in the shape of a Cupid's bow?
   Now you're angry, but—never mind,
   Brother, thy tail hangs down behind!

Here we sit in a branchy row,
Thinking of beautiful things we know;   10
Dreaming of deeds that we mean to do,
All complete, in a minute or two—
Something noble and grand and good,
Won by merely wishing we could.
   Now we're going to—never mind,   15
   Brother, thy tail hangs down behind!

All the talk we ever have heard
Uttered by bat or beast or bird—
Hide or fin or scale or feather—
Jabber it quickly and all together!   20
Excellent! Wonderful! Once again!
Now we are talking just like men.
   Let's pretend we are . . . never mind,
   Brother, thy tail hangs down behind!
   This is the way of the Monkey-kind!   25

Then join our leaping lines that scumfish through the pines,
That rocket by where, light and high, the wild-grape
   swings.
By the rubbish in our wake, and the noble noise we make,
Be sure, be sure, we're going to do some splendid things.

RUDYARD KIPLING
(1865-1936)

1. Who are the Bandar-Log, and what is the meaning of
   lines 1-4?
2. How do you explain lines 7 and 8 of each stanza?
3. What do you like best in the poem?

Notes: page 127.

GOLLYWOG

Gollywog
Is a dirty dog :
  His face is as black as coal,
But his skin's as white
As the pale moonlight
  Compared with the state of his soul.
Who was it broke the sewing-machine ?
  Who was it spilt the ink ?
Who was it pushed the plasticine
  Down the nursery sink ?
Who was it pulled the horsehair out
  From the seat of the best armchair ?
Gollywog did it, there isn't a doubt—
  Nobody else was there.

Gollywog
Is a dirty dog ;
  He's steeped in original sin
From his jet-black hair
To his set black stare
  And his bold and shameless grin.
Who rubbed coal on the mantelpiece ?
  Who spread jam on the floor ?
Who stuffed pellets of candle-grease
  In the lock of the bathroom door ?
Who put jam in Marmaduke's hat
  And butter in Mary's hair ?
Gollywog did it, I'm sure of that—
  Nobody else would dare.

JAN STRUTHER
(20*th Century*)

(Reproduced by permission of the Proprietors of " Punch ".)

1. How old do you think the speaker of this poem is ?
2. In stanzas 2 and 4, lines 1, 2, 3 and 5 all begin with " who ".
   Do you think that is good ?
3. The first stanza might be written thus :
     Gollywog is a dirty dog :
     His face is as black as coal,
     But his skin's as white as the pale moonlight
     Compared with the state of his soul.
   Would it make any difference ?
4. Who was it broke the sewing-machine and did all the
   other things ?

Notes : page 127.

A MIRACULOUS PASSAGE IN HAMELEN

This made me think upon that miraculous passage
in Hamelen, a town in Germany, which I hoped to
have passed through when I was in Hamburg, had we
returned by Holland ; which was thus (nor would I
relate it unto you were there not some ground of truth
for it) : The said town of Hamelen was annoyed with
Rats and Mice ; and it chanced that a Pied-coated
Piper came thither who covenanted with the chief
Burghers for such a reward if he could free them quite
from the said Vermin, nor would he demand it till a
twelve-month, and a day after. The agreement being
made he began to play on his Pipes and all the Rats
and the Mice followed him to a great lough hard by,
where they all perished ; so the Town was infected no
more. At the end of the year the Pied-Piper returned
for his reward ; the Burghers put him off with slightings
and neglect, offering him some small matter, which
he refusing and staying some days in the Town, on
Sunday morning at High Mass, when most people
were at church, fell to play on his Pipes, and all the
children up and down followed him out of the Town
to a great Hill not far off, which rent in two and opened,
and let him and the children in and so closed up again.
This happened a matter of 250 years since, and in that
town they date their Bills and Bonds and other
Instruments in law to this day from the year of the
going out of their children. Besides there is a great
pillar of stone at the foot of the said Hill whereon
this story is engraven.

JAMES HOWELL
(1594-1666)

passage : *happening, event*

This account comes from a letter written by Howell during
a Continental tour.

THE LEGEND OF THE PIED PIPER

Browning's poem has made the story of the Pied Piper known throughout the English-speaking world. To-day we read and enjoy the swift and gaily-coloured verses much as we would a fairy tale, and do not trouble to ask ourselves to what extent, if at all, they may be founded on actual fact. But in Germany, and particularly in Hamelin, people still believe that the piper really came to the town on 26th June, 1284, and stole away a hundred and thirty children. In June, 1934, the six-hundred and-fiftieth anniversary of his visit was duly observed.

Some people, of course, consider the tale is all untrue, or, at most, that it turns an old, wide-spread belief into an account of an actual occurrence. They say that similar stories are told of other places in Europe, and even of Abyssinia. The piper, they explain, is merely the wind, which sets trees and flowers dancing and capering, and which long, long ago was thought to carry with it the souls of the dead.

But the town records of Hamelin told of a real calamity. Inscriptions on public buildings referred to it, and for centuries legal documents were dated from " the year of the Exodus of the Children ". No sound of drum was permitted in " Pied Piper's Street ", and even bridal processions had to pass through it in silence.

In 1655 Pastor Samuel Erich wrote a history of the disappearance of the children, though he said nothing of the mayor's refusal to pay the piper his price for destroying the rats. Browning probably found his story in a book by R. Verstegan which gives all the details as we know them—the broken bargain, the escape of the lame boy, and the explanation of the strange tribe in Transylvania. Learned writers have examined all the evidence that still remains, and have decided that there must be some foundation for a story

that has been accepted so firmly in Hamelin. They
suggest that long ago, when there was no written
history, two noteworthy events became confused in
people's memories—a rat-charming, and a robbery of
children, perhaps by enemies of the city—and that
one strange visitor was at length made responsible for
both.

The legend remains, and will remain, for Browning
has given it new life. He has taken away its gloom.
His children are no longer led off by a fiend to a terrible
fate, but by a piper to a new country,

> *Where waters gushed and fruit trees grew*
> *And flowers put forth a fairer hue.*

THE PIED PIPER OF HAMELIN

I

Hamelin Town's in Brunswick,
  By famous Hanover city;
The river Weser, deep and wide,
Washes its walls on the southern side;
A pleasanter spot you never spied;
  But, when begins my ditty,
Almost five hundred years ago,
To see the townsfolk suffer so
  From vermin, was a pity.

II

  Rats!
They fought the dogs and killed the cats,
  And bit the babies in the cradles,
And ate the cheeses out of the vats,
  And licked the soup from the cooks' own ladles.
Split open the kegs of salted sprats,
Made nests inside men's Sunday hats,
And even spoiled the women's chats
  By drowning their speaking
  With shrieking and squeaking
In fifty different sharps and flats.

III

At last the people in a body
  To the Town Hall came flocking:
" 'Tis clear," cried they, " our Mayor's a noddy;
  And as for our Corporation—shocking
To think we buy gowns lined with ermine
For dolts that can't or won't determine
What's best to rid us of our vermin!
You hope, because you're old and obese,
To find in the furry civic robe ease?
Rouse up, sirs! Give your brains a racking
To find the remedy we're lacking,
Or, sure as fate, we'll send you packing!"
At this the Mayor and Corporation
Quaked with a mighty consternation.

IV

An hour they sat in council.   35
  At length the Mayor broke silence :
" For a guilder I'd my ermine gown sell,
  I wish I were a mile hence !
It's easy to bid one rack one's brain—
I'm sure my poor head aches again,   40
I've scratched it so, and all in vain.
Oh for a trap, a trap, a trap ! "
Just as he said this, what should hap
At the chamber door but a gentle tap ?
" Bless us," cried the Mayor, " what's that ? "   45
(With the Corporation as he sat,
Looking little though wondrous fat ;
Nor brighter was his eye, nor moister
Than a too-long-opened oyster,
Save when at noon his paunch grew mutinous   50
For a plate of turtle, green and glutinous.)
" Only a scraping of shoes on the mat ?
Anything like the sound of a rat
Makes my heart go pit-a-pat ! "

V

" Come in ! " the Mayor cried, looking bigger :   55
And in did come the strangest figure !
His queer long coat from heel to head
Was half of yellow and half of red,
And he himself was tall and thin,
With sharp blue eyes, each like a pin,   60
And light loose hair, yet swarthy skin,
No tuft on cheek nor beard on chin,
But lips where smiles went out and in ;
There was no guessing his kith and kin :
And nobody could enough admire   65
The tall man and his quaint attire.
Quoth one : " It's as my great-grandsire,
Starting up at the Trump of Doom's tone,
Had walked this way from his painted tombstone ! "

78

VI

He advanced to the council table: 70
And, " Please your honours," said he, " I'm able,
By means of a secret charm, to draw
   All creatures living beneath the sun,
   That creep or swim or fly or run,
After me so as you never saw!   75
And I chiefly use my charm
On creatures that do people harm,
The mole and toad and newt and viper;
And people call me the Pied Piper."
(And here they noticed round his neck   80
   A scarf of red and yellow stripe,
To match with his coat of the self-same check;
   And at the scarf's end hung a pipe;
And his fingers, they noticed, were ever straying
As if impatient to be playing   85
Upon this pipe, as low it dangled
Over his vesture so old-fangled.)
" Yet," said he, " poor piper as I am,
In Tartary I freed the Cham,
   Last June, from his huge swarms of gnats;   90
I eased in Asia the Nizam
   Of a monstrous brood of vampyre-bats:
And as for what your brain bewilders,
   If I can rid your town of rats,
Will you give me a thousand guilders? "   95
" One? fifty thousand! "—was the exclamation
Of the astonished Mayor and Corporation.

VII

Into the street the Piper stept,
   Smiling first a little smile,
As if he knew what magic slept   100
   In his quiet pipe the while;
Then, like a musical adept,
To blow the pipe his lips he wrinkled,
And green and blue his sharp eyes twinkled,
Like a candle-flame where salt is sprinkled;   105

And ere three shrill notes the pipe uttered,
You heard as if an army muttered;
And the muttering grew to a grumbling;
And the grumbling grew to a mighty rumbling;
And out of the houses the rats came tumbling.   110
Great rats, small rats, lean rats, brawny rats,
Brown rats, black rats, grey rats, tawny rats,
Grave old plodders, gay young friskers,
    Fathers, mothers, uncles, cousins,
Cocking tails and pricking whiskers,   115
    Families by tens and dozens,
Brothers, sisters, husbands, wives—
Followed the Piper for their lives.
From street to street he piped, advancing,
And step by step they followed dancing,   120
Until they came to the river Weser,
    Wherein all plunged and perished!
—Save one, who, stout as Julius Cæsar,
Swam across and lived to carry
    (As he, the manuscript he cherished)   125
To Rat-land home his commentary:
Which was, " At the first shrill notes of the pipe,
I heard a sound as of scraping tripe,
And putting apples, wondrous ripe,
Into a cider-press's gripe: 130
And a moving away of pickle-tub-boards,
And a leaving ajar of conserve-cupboards,
And a drawing the corks of train-oil flasks,
And a breaking the hoops of butter-casks:
And it seemed as if a voice   135
    (Sweeter far than by harp or by psaltery
Is breathed) called out, ' Oh rats, rejoice!
    The world is grown to one vast drysaltery!
So munch on, crunch on, take your nuncheon,
Breakfast, supper, dinner, luncheon!'   140
And just as a bulky sugar-puncheon,
All ready staved, like a great sun shone
Glorious scarce an inch before me,
Just as methought it said, ' Come, bore me!'
—I found the Weser rolling o'er me."   145

VIII

You should have heard the Hamelin people
Ringing the bells till they rocked the steeple.
" Go," cried the Mayor, " and get long poles,
Poke out the nests and block up the holes !
Consult with carpenters and builders,   150
And leave in our town not even a trace
Of the rats ! "—when suddenly, up the face
Of the Piper perked in the market-place,
With a, " First, if you please, my thousand guilders ! "

IX

A thousand guilders ! The Mayor looked blue ;   155
So did the Corporation too.
For council dinners made rare havoc
With Claret, Moselle, Vin-de-Grave, Hock ;
And half the money would replenish
Their cellar's biggest butt with Rhenish.   160
To pay this sum to a wandering fellow
With a gipsy coat of red and yellow !
" Beside," quoth the Mayor, with a knowing wink,
" Our business was done at the river's brink ;
We saw with our eyes the vermin sink,   165
And what's dead can't come to life, I think.
So, friend, we're not the folks to shrink
From the duty of giving you something for drink,
And a matter of money to put in your poke ;
But, as for the guilders, what we spoke   170
Of them, as you very well know, was in joke.
Beside, our losses have made us thrifty.
A thousand guilders ! Come, take fifty ! "

X

The Piper's face fell, and he cried :
" No trifling ! I can't wait, beside !   175

I've promised to visit by dinner time
Bagdat, and accept the prime
Of the Head-Cook's pottage, all he's rich in,
For having left, in the Caliph's kitchen,
Of a nest of scorpions no survivor :   180
With him I proved no bargain-driver ;
With you, don't think I'll bate a stiver !
And folks who put me in a passion
May find me pipe after another fashion."

XI

" How ? " cried the Mayor, " d'ye think I brook   185
Being worse treated than a Cook ?
Insulted by a lazy ribald
With idle pipe and vesture piebald ?
You threaten us, fellow ? Do your worst ;
Blow your pipe there till you burst ! "   190

XII

Once more he stept into the street,
   And to his lips again
   Laid his long pipe of smooth straight cane ;
And ere he blew three notes (such sweet
Soft notes as yet musician's cunning   195
   Never gave the enraptured air)
There was a rustling, that seemed like a bustling
Of merry crowds justling at pitching and hustling,
Small feet were pattering, wooden shoes clattering,
Little hands clapping, and little tongues chattering ;   200
And, like fowls in a farm-yard when barley is scattering,
Out came the children running.
All the little boys and girls,
With rosy cheeks and flaxen curls,
And sparkling eyes and teeth like pearls,   205
Tripping and skipping, ran merrily after
The wonderful music with shouting and laughter.

XIII

The Mayor was dumb, and the Council stood
As if they were changed into blocks of wood,
Unable to move a step, or cry   210
To the children merrily skipping by,
—Could only follow with the eye
That joyous crowd at the Piper's back.
But how the Mayor was on the rack,
And the wretched Council's bosoms beat,   215
As the Piper turned from the High Street
To where the Weser rolled its waters
Right in the way of their sons and daughters!
However, he turned from South to West,
And to Koppelberg Hill his steps addressed,   220
And after him the children pressed;
Great was the joy in every breast.
" He never can cross that mighty top!
He's forced to let the piping drop,
And we shall see our children stop!"   225
When, lo, as they reached the mountain-side,
A wondrous portal opened wide,
As if a cavern was suddenly hollowed;
And the Piper advanced and the children followed;
And when all were in to the very last,   230
The door in the mountain-side shut fast.
Did I say, all? No! One was lame,
    And could not dance the whole of the way;
And in after years, if you would blame
    His sadness, he was used to say,   235
" It's dull in our town since my playmates left!
I can't forget that I'm bereft
Of all the pleasant sights they see,
Which the Piper also promised me.
For he led us, he said, to a joyous land,   240
Joining the town and just at hand,
Where waters gushed and fruit-trees grew
And flowers put forth a fairer hue,
And everything was strange and new;

The sparrows were brighter than peacocks here,   245
And their dogs outran our fallow deer,
And honey-bees had lost their stings,
And horses were born with eagles' wings:
And just as I became assured
My lame foot would be speedily cured,   250
The music stopped and I stood still,
And found myself outside the hill,
Left alone against my will,
To go now limping as before,
And never hear of that country more!"   255

XIV

Alas, alas for Hamelin!
    There came into many a burgher's pate
    A text which says that heaven's gate
    Opes to the rich at as easy rate
As the needle's eye takes a camel in!   260
The Mayor sent East, West, North, and South,
To offer the Piper, by word of mouth,
    Wherever it was men's lot to find him,
Silver and gold to his heart's content,
If he'd only return the way he went,   265
    And bring the children behind him.
But when they saw 'twas a lost endeavour,
And Piper and dancers were gone for ever,
They made a decree that lawyers never
    Should think their records dated duly   270
If, after the day of the month and year,
These words did not as well appear,
"And so long after what happened here
    On the Twenty-second of July,
Thirteen hundred and seventy-six:"   275
And the better in memory to fix
The place of the children's last retreat,
They called it the Pied Piper's Street—
Where any one playing on pipe or tabor
Was sure for the future to lose his labour,   280

Nor suffered they hostelry or tavern
  To shock with mirth a street so solemn;
But opposite the place of the cavern
  They wrote the story on a column,
And on the great church-window painted   285
The same, to make the world acquainted
How their children were stolen away;
And there it stands to this very day.
And I must not omit to say
That in Transylvania there's a tribe   290
Of alien people who ascribe
The outlandish ways and dress
On which their neighbours lay such stress,
To their fathers and mothers having risen
Out of some subterraneous prison   295
Into which they were trepanned
Long time ago in a mighty band
Out of Hamelin town in Brunswick land,
But how or why, they don't understand.

XV

So, Willy, let me and you be wipers   300
Of scores out with all men—especially pipers!
And, whether they pipe us free from rats or from mice,
If we've promised them aught, let us keep our promise!

BROWNING
(1812-1889)

This is a good story and you should try to enjoy it just as a good story. Look then at one or two points in Browning's art, his manner of telling, and you will find you enjoy the poem still more. We shall deal only with stanzas II and VII.

1. Compare stanza II, lines 11-20, with stanza VII, lines 106-118.
2. What is the effect of line 10?
3. In stanza VII note how often the rhymes are double or even treble. Which set of rhymes in this stanza do you like best?
4. Compare the description of the feast in stanza VII, lines 127-145, with that in the "Song of the Brown Sea Rat", page 59, lines 25-32.

Notes : page 128.

85

NOTES ON THE POEMS

The numbers in brackets after the titles refer to the pages on which the poems appear.

Unlike questions in arithmetic, questions on poetry may frequently have more than one right answer. When you differ from the notes, be ready to support your own opinion.

OFF THE GROUND (10)

1. We should still have known they were jolly farmers. Only jolly men would make such a bet. It was a jolly dance they danced, with " fingers a-flicking " and " knees well bent ". As we read on, our ears tell us the lines of the poem are running to a jolly tune or rhythm which tells us in its own way that this is a light-hearted story. But the word " jolly ", coming, as it does, in the very first line, strikes a happy keynote. We know at once that this is a cheerful poem, and we are ready to follow it in the right mood.

2. Yes. Think of the wonder of the mermaids' home, " the feasting and dancing and minstrelsy " (lines 91-92). Turvey was the most adventurous of the three, the one who would best enjoy the new life under the sea.

3. The poem does not tell us. The story comes to an end with Bates and Giles paying their " forty shilling ". Those who would like to bring Turvey back may try to tell his story in a companion poem. Here is a possible beginning :

   'Twas long, long years
   Beneath the foam
   Ere Turvey thought
   Again of home.

4. See lines 13-15. We are not told very much, but it seems to be a silent, sunny afternoon in Summer, a day on which one might well dance "in dream " (line 48). Perhaps there is a light breeze to ripple the sea (lines 95-96) and make conditions a little more pleasant for the dancers.

5. Lines 11-12. It was " not too fast and not too slow ".
   Lines 31-32. It was " lightsome, but not too quick ".
   Lines 46-52. It was steady as a sleeping top, or an old grandfather clock.

   The rhythm of the poem suggests a dance.

6. The short lines help us to feel that we are dancing with the farmers, right foot, left foot, "not too fast and not too slow", the proper pace for a summer afternoon. The long lines seem to hurry on, in a more bustling, everyday fashion. Note how the phrase "off the ground" loses its force and unexpectedness in the long line.

7. Read again notes 4, 5, 6.
Lines 1-56.   We shall try to keep time with the farmers.
Lines 57-60.   We may try to give a hint of excitement at the sight of the sea.
Lines 61-68.   We may imitate the farmers' speech.
Lines 69-72.   We may suggest something of Turvey's dash.
Lines 73-92.   Can we bring out the mystery and the wonder?
The last lines may be taken more slowly and quietly.
Note that lines 111 and 113 are longer than the others.
Above all, we must remember that they were *jolly* farmers, and read with a sense of fun.

8. The title applies to all that happens in the poem. Each farmer hoped to dance his companions "off the ground", that is, to a stand-still, until they no longer held their ground as dancers. And Farmer Turvey danced Bates and Giles off the ground in quite another and unexpected fashion.
The poem, too, is "off the ground", in the sense that it is unusual, off the beaten track. It is because poetry can often take us away from the ordinary things of life, up into the strange and beautiful worlds of our imaginations, that the title of this poem has been given to the whole book.

✻   ✻   ✻

THE FIDDLE (14)

1. (a) *Over The Hills and Far Away*. The words as we say them have a magic sound, and seem to promise to each of us adventure in strange, mysterious places. So, not only does the fiddler go up the lone hill road, but he goes far away in another sense, far away from ordinary life to the companionship of the furry folk, the birds of the moor and the "wee folk", as the fairies are sometimes called.
(b) The first stanza gave him the "swing" or rhythm of his poem. Note how good a rhythm it is for a fiddle tune and a fairy dance.

2. It was a "darling song" (line 24), so bonny that he had no wish to learn another (lines 4-5), a fairy air (line 32) with magic in it to gather birds and beasts and fairies around him, to set feet dancing and dancers chuckling with glee (line 27).

88

3. *Zig-a-zig-zig.*

If the word stood all by itself, we could stress it as we cared, but here the dancing rhythm of the poem compels us to take it in one way. In the following stanza the sleepy rhythm compels us to take it in the other :

Velvet curtains, glowing embers,

Couches soft and deep,

Fiddles' drowsy zig-a-zig-zig

Summon gentle sleep.

4. No ! This is a tune for wee folk and quick feet. Say aloud :

Three jolly Farmers

Once bet a pound

Each dance the other would

Off the ground.

Then say :

And oh ! how they chuckled with elfin glee

To the zig-a-zig-zig of my minstrelsy !

Do you note how different they are ?

5. Line 19.   Where is the fiddler ?
   Lines 20-22.   What is the scene at his feet ?
   Lines 9, 13, 18.   Who are his companions ?
   Lines 23-24, or 33-35.   What are they doing ?
   The fiddler was young and light-hearted, " the Captain of that band ".
   Now paint your picture.

6. See note 1.   Remember the fiddle took the fiddler and his friends " far away ", out of the glen, through the woods, on to the moor, up and up to the lone hill road among the rushes and fern.
   Line 40.   Now his happiness is gone, never to come back.   The drum makes a brave noise, but it cannot call the fairies.

7. Yes !   It takes us away into a strange and happy world, quite different from the one we know.   Poetry often offers us a magic carpet of this kind.   Read in this book, for example, " The Wee Wee Man " (page 30), " Puk-Wudjies " (page 32), " The Little Young Lambs " (page 46), " Sam " (page 62).

89

1. (*a*) Seamen in from the sea are on holiday there.

   (*b*) The air is full of the music of bells. If we are not actually hearing bells, we are talking about them all through the poem.
   Find one line (there is one) which does not refer to bells and the ringing of bells.

2. " Boom " and " beat " (line 6), " a-jangle " (line 15), " booming " (line 19), " clangs " (line 20).

3. (*a*) He has used many words which have a bell-like sound, *e.g.* " lagoon " (line 2), " chime ", " jingle " (line 3). You will find it easy to complete the list.

   (*b*) He has brought similar sounds close together, like a bell's ding-dong—" rh*yme* " and " ch*ime* " (line 5), " boom " and " *beat* " (line 6), " *sonsie seamen* " (line 11), " *beaten bells* come *booming* " (lines 18-19).

   (*c*) He writes in a " ding-dong " rhythm, and every now and again he beats out the tune for us :

> *The bells they chime and jingle*
>
> *From dawn to afternoon.*
>
> *They rhyme and chime and mingle,*
>
> *They pulse and boom and beat,*
>
> *And the laughing bells are gentle*
>
> *And the mournful bells are sweet.*

   Now mark the " beats " in lines 14, 15, 16, 20.

   (*d*) The last lines of the poem re-echo the first lines. As we read them we seem to hear the same notes ring out over and over again. Have you listened to bell-music from a church tower or on the radio ?

4. The sound of line 5 seems to tell us that those bells are smaller and higher in tone. They are, perhaps, the laughing bells (line 7).
   In line 6 we hear the deeper and slower note of the mournful bells (line 8).

5. We shall try to bring out the bell-music, read the poem at not too fast a speed, and pay full attention to the sound of every word. Let us imagine we hear bells ringing out over the still waters of the lagoon, and try to read to their music.

1. See lines 29-32 and 35-38. Like the minstrels of earlier times, he has tales of battle, of love, of fairies and goblins—the themes that interest us still. Again, like the old minstrels, he is ready to tell the history of the family that is prepared to give him a hearing. Such tales were preserved only in memory. Not for hundreds of years, perhaps, were they written down, but the men and women who heard them would tell them to their children, who would at a later date pass them on in their turn. " The Wee Wee Man " and " The Lowlands of Holland " (pages 30, 64) must for long have been kept alive by telling, not by writing.

2. The minstrel has a manly voice (line 5), but he tells us he is no rough soldier. His art is to touch gentle hearts with his lays; and his tales of love and fairies may be better than his songs of war and his legends of Rokeby's warlike lords.

3. A wizard is a magician. So, too, is a poet, who can carry us to strange places, " over the hills and far away ", bring before us people who never existed in the flesh and make them more real than our actual neighbours. He can make us love or hate at will, be happy or sad, soothe us with quiet lines or rouse us to excitement.

4. The times were difficult, and he had the safety of his lady to consider. He felt that it was no night to admit wandering strangers to Rokeby. We may infer, also, that he was not especially interested in songs and tales such as the minstrel offered. Their " magic" did not appeal to him. He was stern (line 13) and all unmoved by the singer's gentle plea.

5. (a) Summer eve is gone and past,
    Summer dew is falling fast;
    I have wandered all the day,
    Do not bid me farther stray!
    Gentle hearts, of gentle kin,
    Take the wandering harper in!

    (b) The king wants soldiers; war, I trow,
    Were meeter trade for such as thou.
    Depart in peace, with Heaven to guide;
    If longer by the gate thou dwell,
    Trust me, thou shalt not part so well.

You will note that in each line there are four stresses or " beats ",
and that in each line the stress or " beat " falls on every second syllable.
But in (*a*) the stressed syllable comes before the unstressed, so that the
line runs

> tum-*ti* tum-*ti* tum-*ti* tum.

In (*b*) the unstressed syllable comes first. and the line runs

> *ti*-tum *ti*-tum *ti*-tum *ti*-tum.

Quite apart from the things the speakers say, the minstrel's speech
sounds more gentle, more appealing. The porter commands, and the
rhythm of his lines is sharp and emphatic.

6. See note 5. The minstrel may chant his lines, as though to a harp
accompaniment. The porter will reply with vigour. Remember that
both speakers are some distance away from the company in the hall.
It might be well in the reading to place minstrel and porter where the
audience can hear, but not see them.

*   *   *

THE TOY BAND (20)

1. Only spirited, good marching tunes would have roused the stragglers.
And as we listen to the poem, particularly the second half of each stanza,
a lively marching tune rings in our ears.

> *Rubadub! Rubadub! Wake and take the road again,*
> *Wheedle-deedle-deedle-dee, come, boys, come!*
> *You that mean to fight it out, wake and take your load again,*
> *Fall in! Fall in! Follow the fife and drum!*

We might take the last line :

> *Fall in! Fall in!*

Which reading do you prefer?

See " The Minstrel at the Gate ", note 5 (page 91).

2. The Big Dragoon " marched round and round the fountain ", " beating
the drum like mad " (see page 22), and, no doubt, playing the same
tune over and over again. The poet expresses something of this
determination by repeating the lines, and, in a way, marches us round
and round, too.

Just as the repetition of the tunes roused the soldiers, so the repetition
of those lines rouses us. Each time we hear them we become keener
in spirit, more ready to rise and march to the tune.

92

Each repetition fits perfectly into the story and helps to carry it **on**. In stanza 1 the lines tell us what the Big Dragoon wished to play; in stanza 2 what he did play; in stanza 3 they lift the feet of the soldiers along the road; in stanza 4 they seem to lift *our* feet, to urge us to " fight it out ".

Everyone likes a chorus, even if the words have little meaning. Here they have meaning and force.

3. (*a*) We must remember that here we have a marching rhythm, and see to it that the lines march as we say them. See note 1.

(*b*) Each stanza must be considered by itself. We must mark the change from dejection to triumph.

(*c*) It would be possible to employ three speakers—a narrator to take the first four lines of each stanza, a " drummer " to take the fifth line, a " whistler " to take the sixth. The last two lines may be taken by " drummer " and " whistler " together, or with good effect by the whole class.

*   *   *

THE TOY BAND and THE RETREAT FROM MONS (20, 21)

1.

PROSE	POEM
The Scene	
The town was St. Quentin, on the le Cateau road. It was protected by a river, the bridge over which was held by troops and machine guns. The stragglers were some in houses and others round the fountain in the Square.	The town is unnamed. It was dreary.
The Time	
The troops were not clear of the town till midnight.	It was dark.
The Troops	
They were marched off their feet and straggled into the town in a demoralised condition. They lay about in the streets and in the houses and round the fountain like the dead. The few officers in the town could not rouse them.	Stragglers lay wearily about, like dead men.

93

Sir Tom Bridges wished for a band. A toy-shop supplied his trumpeter and himself with a tin whistle and a drum. They marched round and round the fountain, playing ' The British Grenadiers ' and ' Tipperary ', and beating the drum like mad. When the men sat up, Sir Tom Bridges urged them to make an effort, and promised to lead them back to their regiments. They moved off slowly to the music of whistle and drum and a couple of mouth organs.

The Big Dragoon wished for a drum and a fife. He found a drum and a penny whistle in a toy-shop. By means of these the men were persuaded to march.

2. Check this for yourself from note 1.

You will find that the prose gives many more details—the name of the town, its position, the time, the lack of officers to lead the men, the " musicians " and the tunes they played, the exhortation made to the troops.

Sir Tom Bridges is writing an accurate history of the occurrence, and his aim is to put everything clearly before us.

3. The poet's aim is different from the historian's. He has been, himself, deeply moved by the story, and he wishes us to share his feelings. For him, therefore, there are two important facts, and two only :

(1) The troops were " down ", " dead men " ;

(2) The music of a penny whistle and a toy drum brought their spirit back.

We have read in " The Fiddle " (page 14) of a magic tune that charmed beast and bird and fairy. Here is another that charmed " dead men " to life.

The poet tells us the road was long and the town was dreary, because the triumph of whistle and drum is seen thereby to be all the more splendid. The name of the town, the exact time of the night, even the names of the tunes that were played would not have made the triumph any greater or more thrilling to us.

4. We may select the following phrases and titles :
Stanza 1. " Weary lay the stragglers " . . . Despair.
Stanza 2. " Here's a drum ! " . . . . Hope.
Stanza 3. " Cheerly goes the dark road " . . Triumph.
Stanza 4. " We'll not forget " . . . . Praise.

5. Stanza 4. The story is told in stanzas 1-3 of the poem. But the poet wishes us to feel as strongly as possible his delight in the courage of the Big Dragoon and the spirit of the soldiers. See note 3. We admire the quiet modesty with which Sir Tom Bridges tells his story, but, like the poet, we wish to say, " Well done ! " and we are glad the poem gives us the chance to say it.

THE KNIGHT'S LEAP (24)

1. The aim of the prose is to tell the story like history, step by step, from the knight's oppression of the city to his death-leap into the glen. As it tells us, first of all, of the harrying of the burghers, our sympathies are with them in their fight. It tells the story of the knight's leap quietly and in the third person.

The poet's aim is different. He is interested in one part of the story, the death of the knight. He begins, accordingly, quite abruptly, with his defeat, and leaves us to piece together the previous events.

In the prose there is no attempt to make the knight's death seem grand and heroic. We feel that such an end was better than hanging, but we feel that his fate was well deserved.

Because the poet is interested only in the knight, he brings him before us in person, lets him tell his own story, and in the telling reveal his own reckless, fearless nature. We are on his side from the first line. We see his past life through his eyes and share his contempt for his foes. We feel it right that he should die as he has lived, in the saddle. He is old, his horse is old, and it is fitting that they should die together. Only once does the knight refer to his raids on the city—when he calls himself " the Altenahr hawk ".

The prose tells us the bare story. The poem describes. From it we can make pictures for ourselves of the knight and the scene within the castle.

Compare the two accounts of the leap. The poem adds those details that make us see the picture—the clear moonshine, the mounting of the horse, the spurring, the tight rein, the wall, the cliff, the darkness below.

Note how the repetition of " out " in lines 24-25 seems to add to the splendour of the leap. Compare them with, " He leaped him over the wall and cliff, into the darkness ". All the glory has gone.

Poetry has in its rhymes and its rhythms—the swing of its lines—a power of stirring our feelings that prose has not. Consider lines 9-10. Every word is a single syllable, yet, as we read them aloud, all the courage and the pride of the knight ring out.

There is little difference between the actual words used in poem and prose. On the whole, those of the poem are shorter. Note how few there are of more than one syllable, only one per line in the first stanza. Certain words and phrases of the prose we should not expect to find in the poem, e.g. " gradually ", " besiegers ", " progress ", " water supply ". Certain words of the poem are not commonly found in prose, e.g. " harness " (armour), " tree " (gallows), " borne " (carried), " of yore " (in the past).

2. Each method is good in its own way. If we wish to have all the facts, we shall prefer the plain and orderly prose. But if we wish a vivid and stirring tale, one that will live in our memories, we shall choose the poem.

3. See note 1. The castle will stand out in the clear moonshine. There may be a fiery gleam from the burning gate. The central figures will be those of the mail-clad knight and his horse as they leap out into the darkness below.

4. Here is a possible stanza:

> *Nor corn they reaped, nor wine they pressed;*
> *Like hawks they fell from the sky;*
> *Till the burghers said, " We will harry their nest,*
> *For we or the hawks must die ".*

*   *   *

LEEZIE LINDSAY and ALLEN-A-DALE (26)

1. At first sight the stanzas may seem to be much alike. Both have four lines, rhyme, and regular rhythm. In their first three lines there is a difference of one word only.
But consider those words. The " pictures " are a commonplace, and a visit to the " pictures " is an ordinary, every-day occurrence. The word " Highlands " has magic in it, the power to excite us.
Still more magical and exciting is the invitation to be a " bride and a darling " compared with one to have tea at the baker's.
Let us remember that rhyme and regular rhythm, by themselves, do not make a poem.

> *As with my hat upon my head*
> *I walked along the Strand,*
> *I there did meet another man*
> *With his hat in his hand.*

Those lines do not excite us, do not lift us above the every-day things of life. They are not poetry, but doggerel.
Contrast them with the following:

> *I met a lady in the meads,*
> *Full beautiful, a faery's child,*
> *Her hair was long, her foot was light,*
> *And her eyes were wild.*

Do you *feel* the difference?

2. He is an outlaw, a dweller in the greenwood, as was Robin Hood in days gone by.

3. Why did we sympathise with the knight, and not with the burghers of Altenahr? See " The Knight's Leap ", note 1, page 95.

We know Allen much better than we know the Baron of Ravensworth and his lady. He is the right type of hero, brave, ready in reply, good-looking and charming.

Lines 11-12.   We are glad to hear that he is free of all the living things in the Baron's dominions.

Lines 21-24.   We delight in his triumph over the careful mother.

Note how the word " prance " (line 7) at once causes us to dislike the Baron, and how the mother's interest in houses and wealth places her in our minds beside her worldly husband.

Note, too, the quick and spirited rhythm in which the poem is written :

Allen-a-Dale has no fagot for burning,
Allen-a-Dale has no furrow for turning.

As soon as we have caught the swing of it in our reading, we are in tune with Allen, and are carried by the dashing lines to live with him in the greenwood and share in his success.

4. See note 2.   The hero's very name has a cheerful sound.   The rhythm is cheerful.   The first three lines have certainly prepared us for the good news of line 4.

5. Both girls have comfortable homes.   Leezie Lindsay dresses in " green satin " that only the well-to-do could buy in Scotland at the time of the song ; and the lass who flees to the forest is a Baron's daughter. Both leave their homes for their lovers.   To some it may seem that Leezie is the more cautious.   She suggests to Lord Ronald in lines 5-8 the question that is actually put to Allen-a-Dale by the mother (line 20), and agrees to set out only when she has received a satisfactory answer. Would you have liked the poem better had lines 11-12 read

My name it is Ronald Macdonald,
And my hame's in the North countree ?

On the other hand, Leezie's question is put in such a way as to show she is already in love with the stranger, and, even though he does prove to be " a chieftain of high degree ", she shows courage and spirit in leaving comfort and safety at his call.   The Highlands have a charm for us to-day.   It was a far and a hard journey to them some two hundred years ago.   Leezie is ready at once (lines 13-14) to set out on foot.

6. This question, like No. 5, is one to which each must give his or her own answer.

" Allen-a-Dale " goes with a swing.   We are carried by the rhythm away from our ordinary, every-day life into the heart of the greenwood. The quick movement from scene to scene makes us feel more keenly still that we are free in the fresh, open air.

Everything is exactly as we should like it to be. We find ourselves in that fine country where a stout heart, a quick wit, and a gay laugh triumph over " steely " and " stony " parents. So much do we delight in Allen's courage and dash, that we imagine we are the hero of the sharp spur and the bright blade, sure of ourselves and ready for whatever may befall.

The story of " Leezie Lindsay " is told in quieter lines, but it, too, takes us into a country of quick action and happy endings. Note (a) how suddenly, in the very first line, we are taken away from ourselves into the lives of the hero and heroine ; (b) how the repetition in lines 1-3 tells us that Lord Ronald is completely in love with Leezie ; and (c) how her readiness to face the difficulties of the road tells us that she is a proper wife for a Highland chieftain.

A story of this kind might well be so " sweet " that it would only bore us, but this is told simply and freshly.

In Lord Ronald's question, Leezie's half-laughing reply, and her bold, quick decision we have all we require not only to learn the story but to picture the characters for ourselves.

We have already spoken of the magic of the " Highlands " (note 1). The word captures us in the very first line.

*   *   *

MY LADY GREENSLEEVES (28)

1. The poem gives us full details of Greensleeves' dress—her green gown with wide sleeves, her belt of gold set with pearls, her skirt of the finest cloth, her crimson stockings and her milk-white shoes. Do you see her on her gay gelding surrounded by her lover's men all in green, or as the harvest queen, or intent upon her music. Is she young ? Does she laugh often ? Are her eyes bright ?

2. The poem rings sweetly in our ears, partly because, like an old-time tune, it is so different from what we are accustomed to hear.
It is simple and direct and honest. The rich lover has certainly wooed his lady with gifts, but lines 9-12 and 45-48 show that his love is sincere enough, and that he still wishes her well.
Again, we may like the brightly coloured picture of a beauty of long ago (note 1). Is not Greensleeves a lovely name for her ?

3. (a) *Alas, my love, you do me wrong*

    To cast me off discourteously ;

  And I have loved you so long,

    Delighting in your company.

98

(b) Allen-a-Dale has no fagot for burning,

Allen-a-Dale has no furrow for turning,

Allen-a-Dale has no fleece for the spinning,

Yet Allen-a-Dale has red gold for the winning.

In " My Lady Greensleeves " you will note that stressed syllables (marked /) and unstressed syllables (marked ⌣) come alternately, so that the lines run

ti-tum *ti*-tum *ti*-tum *ti*-tum.

In " Allen-a-Dale " there are two unstressed syllables for each stressed one, and the line runs

tum-*ti-ti* **tum**-*ti-ti* **tum**-*ti-ti* **tum**-*ti*.

You will agree that the latter runs more lightly, and that the lines sound more spirited and gay, as they should in a spirited poem. Here are the first lines of " My Lady Greensleeves " re-written in **the rhythm** of " Allen-a-Dale " :

Lady, my Love, but you do me a wrong.

You have I loved, you alone, and so long.

Cast me off, can you, discourteously, (/)

Whose only delight was in your company? (/)

They have the same meaning as the first stanza of the poem, but they trip too merrily ever to have come from the lips of the woe-begone lover.

*　　　*　　　*

THE WEE WEE MAN (30)

1. The first picture is bare of colour. " Between a water and a wa' " stands the wee wee man, short, broad-shouldered, stout-limbed, broad-faced. How shall we clothe him—in green, the fairy colour ; in leather, like a dwarf ; in rich attire, like a king ?

In the second picture, the fine ladies, all in green, troop out on the grass. Where do they come from ? Are they wee or tall, dark or fair ? Do they wear jewels and gold chains ?

The third picture is a scene of splendour—the crystal floor, the golden roof, the broad, broad stair. How shall we dress the dancing ladies— in green again ?

99

2. Shall we call it a " true " fairy story ?

The wee wee man seems part of fairyland, as do the beautiful ladies dressed in the fairy colour, and the dancers in the bonny hall. The wee wee man vanishes just as fairies do—in a flash and with no explanation. Compare "The Fiddle", lines 33-36 (page 15).
But the poet makes us feel that he actually saw all he describes. Only once, in lines 11-13, does he suggest that he is astonished. He accepts quietly and without surprise the ladies and the dancers, and so persuades us to accept them, too. He speaks of *the* bonny green, *the* bonny hall, *the* broad, broad stair, *our* horse, *my* wee wee man, as though he had but lately seen them and they were still fresh in his mind. This plain, quiet way of talking of marvellous things makes the poem more mysterious still.

The poem is real in the way a dream is real to the dreamer. Like a dream, it begins suddenly and ends in the twinkling of an eye. As in dreams, we pass from scene to scene ; and the scenes seem to have little connection with each other. There is no explanation of anything that happens, but everything seems natural at the time.

3. No ! That stanza would have explained too much. We should have known how to take the poem, and lost the pleasure of wondering about it. The poem would have become more " ordinary ". Its strangeness, its mystery would have gone.

4. Here you must choose for yourself.

5. *On we leapt, and away we rode.*
We should take the poem quickly. The poet wastes no time in trying to explain, or even in wondering at what he sees. We have noted how suddenly his tale begins and ends. Note, too, how quickly things happen in the course of it. The wee wee man says nothing when we meet him ; he takes up a " mickle stane ". No time is lost in telling us who speaks in lines 13-16, in telling of the horses or the ride, or where the ladies in green come from. Such explanations would have slowed down the pace of the poem and destroyed much of its strangeness. In our reading, " on we leap, and away we ride ".

*   *   *

PUK-WUDJIES (32)

1. We are much more likely to hear them. They live under cover, and keep very close to the ground, in the woods, in the heather, among the grasses of the hay-field, the fallen leaves of Autumn, the roots of the berried hedges. All the poem tells us of their appearance is that they are brown and small (lines 6, 23) but we hear much more about the sounds they make.

2. We are told most clearly in lines 30-35.

3. There is a " rustle " in lines 7-8, and another in lines 10-11. Say them aloud and listen. Perhaps lines 22-23 are the " bumpiest ". " Puk-Wudjies " itself is a " bumpy " word.

4. See lines 30-35. They move about far less regularly than we do, in all sorts of quick and unexpected ways.

5. Certainly the rhythm is not a " walking " one. In the short lines we seem to take little, scurrying runs, and in the long lines we jump. Read each line with two strong " beats ", and you will hear the Puk-Wudjies scurrying and bumping.

> *They live 'neath the curtain*
>
> *Of fir woods and heather,*
>
> *And never take hurt in*
>
> *The wildest of weather,*
>
> *But best they love Autumn—she's brown as themselves—*
>
> *And they are the brownest of all the brown elves.*

Note that each stanza is built up in the same way—four short lines ; two long ; two short ; one long ; two short ; one long.
The rhymes, too, seem to " rustle " and " bump "—" curtain ", " hurt in " ; " heather ", " weather " ; " West Wind ", " best wind " ; " dead leaves ", " red leaves ".

6. Autumn is brown as themselves, the brown season of fallen leaves, the season of windfalls—beech nuts, chestnuts, acorns. She is the season, too, of loud winds and squally showers, of pattering noises such as the Puk-Wudjies make, and of the shadowy gloaming light that they like best.

7. Our Puk-Wudjies are not mischievous. The shy squirrels do not fear them (line 12) and the trees are kind to them (lines 22-24). But they do make rather eerie noises in the Autumn woodlands at twilight.

8. We should read in rather a small voice, and try hard to bring out the " Puk-Wudjie " rhythm (note 5). We must not forget the rustles and bumps (notes 2 and 3). We shall find stanza 3 particularly interesting. Let us think of a wood on a rather dark and " rustly " evening, or of the little noises the house makes when we are all alone in it. We shall read softly with little listening pauses, for those queer wee sounds are very sudden, and very hard to explain.

GRIM and THE HORSEMAN (34)

1. " Grim " is the bigger. Picture the mountains rising high above the valley mists into the wide, wintry sky. Picture the forty fires and the giant sitting in the glare. In the second poem it is as if we look through a tiny gap in a curtained window, and see the horseman only.

2. Neither is easy to paint. The giant is clear in our mind's eye. The poem brings us so near to him that we can even tell that his sheep is " thick-wooled ". Then in the last lines of the poem we are in the sleeping village far below—so far below that every man and woman is fast asleep, and all that the hungry dog can spy is a twinkle of the watch-fire on the peaks. We have really two pictures, cut off, one from the other, by the mists. Can we build them into one, make clear the " giantness " of Grim, and at the same time make clear the height of the mountains and the vast dome of the sky ?
The horseman must be painted very delicately. Note that we hear him before we see him. Is he riding downhill towards us, or uphill and away ? Do we see his face ? Is the landscape bare or wooded ?

3. Both are really still. Grim is so far from the village that no sound reaches it. Even the crackling of his forty fires is as nothing in the great quiet of the mountains under the night sky. We hear the horseman, but the poem itself is so still that we feel the hoof-beats are faint, and that horse and rider go past like visitors from another world.

4. You must decide for yourself. Which seems to you farther away— the world of Grim roasting his supper upon the mountain tops, or the world of the helmed horseman on his ivory horse who comes and is gone silently, in the moonlight ?

*   *   *

THREE CHARMS (35)

1. A good place would be by the fire in a country cottage on a dark winter evening. The people for whom the charms were written lived far from cities : water had to be carried from the well, and roads were dark at night.

2. Surely they should be spoken by a very old, very wise woman, in a still, wise voice.

3. We may feel that the first and second poems are a mixture of magic and sound, every-day advice. We may even wonder if they were first thought of by parents who wished to have clean and tidy children. The third is pure magic. We may imagine boys and girls of long ago facing the real dangers and—even worse—the queer nameless fears that haunt dark and lonely places, because in their hands they clutched each a " holy piece of bread ".

102

GALLOPING DICK (36)

1. The two long stanzas put before us two pictures. In the first we see Galloping Dick swinging up the stony lane, through the trees, over the heath-covered heights of the Chiltern Hills. In the second we see the same slopes a hundred and twenty years later. Trees and brambles have given way to plough-land; houses cluster on the ridge; the stony lane remains, but lovers stroll where the grey mare galloped past. Lines 33-36 present no picture, but suggest a ghostly sound—clattering hoofs still to be heard through the moaning of the night wind. Possible " chapter " titles are:

> The Highwayman's Hill,
> The Hill To-day,
> The Ghostly Rider.

2. In line 15 of the poem we learn that Dick was hanged, and this knowledge is in our minds as we read of the changes on the hill (lines 21-28). The line suggested in the question would hide the hanging from us, and we should follow the second stanza with Dick's triumph still before us, until with a shock we came to line 31. But the poet wishes us to know early in the poem that Dick was hanged. She tells us three times (lines 15, 31, 33) because she has quite another surprise for us—that of lines 34-36.

3. Galloping Dick was brave and suave and quick. Line 16 or 32 is quick, too, much quicker than the line given in the question. Say it aloud and hear the hoofs clatter on the road. It is much more emphatic, also, as though the poet said, " They hanged him, and that was that ! " Compare line 32 with line 36. Was the hanging the end of the story, after all ?

4. *More than a hundred and twenty years ago,*
   Spurring his horse over the heath-clad height,
   Galloping Dick, the reckless knight of the road,
   Time and again came riding hard through the night.

   One hundred and twenty years ago,
   Over the heath-clad height,
   Galloping Dick, the highwayman,
   Came riding through the night.

   Read both versions aloud, and note how much more quick and sharp the lines of the poem are. They are more full of life, the reckless, hard-galloping, highwayman's life that they describe.

5. " Straggles " suggests a winding, old-fashioned, seemingly purposeless road at the foot of the hills—the very road to suit a highwayman's designs. " Glittering " hints at moonshine on the water rippling far below. " Lawless " sums up all that we have learned of the hill as it was in Dick's day, wooded and bramble-grown, unpeopled, the very place to shelter lawless men.

6. We may take pleasure in reading about rogues or in watching their exploits on the screen, though, quite rightly, we have no desire to meet them in actual life. As we read the two long stanzas of the poem, we take pleasure in the speed and the sharp, horse-hoof rattle of the lines, in the brightness of the pictures, and in the contrast between " then " and " now ". The last four lines are pleasing in another way, with their suggestion of the ghostly gallop in the windy night.

7. In the first stanza our guiding words may be Dick's " What care I ? " We should put into our reading all the dash and energy that we can, and mark the hoof-beats clearly.
The second stanza may be taken more slowly and more quietly. Lovers stroll in the lane that echoed to the grey mare's feet.
The last four lines may have just a hint in them of the night-wind's sigh. We should take them quietly and let our voices hint at something strange and eerie.
This poem ask for many changes in tone and pace. But it well repays the thought we give to it.

* * *

THE FOX-CUB (38)

1. Three foxes speak. The innocent and trusting little brother asks his question in the first two lines of each stanza. The cub of the title makes his cock-sure and flowery reply in the next four lines. The old fox says very little, but it is all to the point. He stands for wisdom.

2. No ! Little foxes are not at all likely to mistake the sounds and sights of the hunt, or to talk in highly-coloured language.

3. It is funny. There is good fun in the fox-cub's beautiful pictures of the " farmer-lads " and the children " 'mong the crimsoning leaves ", because the old fox has let us into the secret. There is good fun in the very sudden ending of the third picture in line 21. For the neat effect of lines 8, 16, 24 compare " Galloping Dick ", lines 16, 32.
We have seen already, in note 2, that we are not to take the story seriously, as though it described some actual happening. It comes to a complete end in line 24, and we need have no sad thoughts as to what might happen afterwards.

4. Our fox-cub is very young and very " arty " and opinionated. Had he been a man-cub, he would have worn his hair long and sported remarkable shirts and ties. We laugh at the lines he speaks, not because they are poetry, but because they are false and because he is quite absurd in his ignorance and conceit.

5. The enquiring little fox will speak very respectfully, for he will, no doubt, be impressed by his brother's claims to wisdom. Mr. Know-all will show a strong belief in himself. He will speak his lines with enjoyment and rather slowly, so that his hearer may have the full benefit. But he will become a very ordinary little fox in line 21, the most amusing line in the poem. The old fox is practical. He speaks crisply and to the point.

6. The cub speaks twelve of the twenty-four lines. The old fox speaks very little. The old fox is right, and the cub is wrong, but it is in his mistakes and his conceit that we are interested. He is the subject of the poem.

*　　*　　*

THE TORTOISESHELL CAT (39)

1. Like a sunflower the cat is big and bright. Her coat of orange and black recalls the yellow and brown of the flower.

2. In Genesis, xxxvii, 3, we are told that Joseph's father " made him a coat of many colours ".

3. Do you see Josephine in her shiny coat of orange and black, her white breast, her pink nose, and her sea-green eyes ?

4. Lines 7-10 tell us that Josephine's colours, which shine so brightly in the sun, will be lost in the dark of evening. Lines 17-20 tell us that, too, but they hint at another twilight—the twilight of Josephine's life when she will no longer be gay and smooth and fat.

5. " All is vanity " was a sad thought to Ecclesiastes, because he thought much of the display that men made and the quickness with which their glory passed away. It is a sad thought for us all when we apply it to our own lives. But it becomes amusing, rather than sad, when we apply it to a cat's life, for we are not accustomed to think of cats so seriously. The poet means us to smile. Think of the gay swing of his lines and his many rhymes.

> *The tortoiseshell cat*
>
> *She sits on the mat,*
>
> *As gay as a sunflower she ;*
>
> *In orange and black you see her blink,*
>
> *And her waistcoat's white and her nose is pink,*
>
> *And her eyes are green as the sea.*

See note 5. We may pretend to be solemn, and so bring out the fun more sharply. The first nine lines of each stanza may be taken by one reader, and the tenth with full force and impressiveness by the whole class ; or one reader may take lines 1-6, another, very seriously, lines 7-9, and the class, as before, line 10.

ON A CAT, AGEING (40)

1. Like Josephine, he has a comfortable life, and his loud purrs tell us that he is smooth and fat. But he is beginning to grow old, and Josephine is still in her " brightest day ".

2. We see Josephine more clearly. We are not told anything of this cat's colour, or eyes, or nose.

3. This cat is more interesting. We do not see his skin, but we see into his mind, and thoughts are always more interesting than coats, however gay they be.

4. The lines in the question would take much of the fun out of the poem. They would suggest that the cat knew he was growing less nimble, whereas, as the poet sees him, he is the picture of self-satisfaction. He is quite sure that life for him is always to be one glad, loud purr.

5. Yes. He sees a sleek and comfortable cat, and is struck by the idea—which the cat cannot have—that his happy life will *not* go on for ever. " The Tortoiseshell Cat " declares that " All is vanity ". This poem, which sets down the cat's thoughts, cannot use those actual words, but with great skill the poet makes us feel their truth in his final stanza.

6. Both are amusing. In the first we are pleased by the pretended seriousness of the author, in the second by the study of the cat's mind. The first poem is gay and colourful, the second is subtle, giving us something to think about.

7. For the rhythm of " The Tortoiseshell Cat " see note 5 to that poem. The rhythm of this poem is more sedate.

He blinks upon the hearth-rug
And yawns in deep content,
Accepting all the comforts
That Providence has sent.

This cat is older, more sedate than Josephine.

*   *   *

OLD WINTER (41)

1. Stanza 2 gives the clearest picture of Winter. Do you see him, an old gaunt figure, newly risen from a snow-drift, grimly scowling and thrusting forth a wrinkled hand, as if to beckon the storm ?

2. Stanza 1 : Winter is clad in snow. He makes a doleful din.
   Stanza 3 : He breathes death to grass and flower and tree.
   Stanza 4 : His eyes are hard and cold as icicles.
   Stanza 5 : His bite freezes.

3. (a) *But let him howl till he crack his jowl.*
   (b) *And scowling stand, with his wrinkled hand*
      Outstretching to the storm.
   (c) *Let him push at the door, in the chimney roar,*
      And rattle the window pane.

In (a) " howl " sounds cold and desolate, and the sound is repeated in " jowl ".

In (b) give the " s " and " r " sounds their full force. They help to make us hear the storm.

In (c) the " r " sounds again suggest a blustering wind.

4. *Old Winter, sad in snow yclad,*
   Is making a doleful din;
But let him howl till he crack his jowl,
   We will not let him in.

In lines 1 and 3 a word in the middle of the line rhymes with a word at the end. Such a rhyme is called mid-rhyme.

Examine the other stanzas and you will find mid-rhymes in each first and third line. There are thus six rhyming words in each stanza, and they certainly help to give the cheery, " what care we? " note to the poem. Hear how much we lose in this version of the last stanza:

Come, lads, let's sing till the rafters hear;
   Come, push the can about:
From our snug fire-side this Christmas time
   We'll keep Old Winter out.

Yet only two words have been changed.

5. Read a stanza until you have the rhythm of it in your ear. The first and third lines have each four " beats ", the second and fourth each three.

Let him push at the door, in the chimney roar,

And rattle the window pane;

Let him in at us spy with his icicle eye

But he shall not entrance gain.

Here is a possible stanza:

Let his hail and sleet in a winding-sheet

Wrap up the stars from sight;

Let him smother the moon: we're clear as noon

In our lanterns' shining light.

6. The mood is one of cheerful, singing comradeship. All are good fellows together, and the poem goes with a hearty swing. Lines 19-20 or 21-22 tell us very well how to say it.

<u>EDDI'S SERVICE</u> (42)

1. (*a*) It was in the manger of an ox's stall that Jesus was born.
    And she brought forth her firstborn son, and wrapped him in swaddling clothes, and laid him in a manger ; because there was no room for them in the inn. (Luke, ii, 7.)
   Read the chapter again, verses 1-20.
   (*b*) On an ass Jesus made his triumphal entry into Jerusalem.
    And the disciples went, and did as Jesus commanded them. And brought the ass, and the colt, and put on them their clothes, and they set him thereon.
    And a very great multitude spread their garments in the way ; others cut down branches from the trees, and strawed them in the way.
                                    (Matthew, xxi, 6-8.)
   Read the chapter again, verses 1-11.
2. The stanzas that present pictures most clearly are probably Nos. 4, 5, and 9. Choose the lines that appeal most strongly to you. Try to picture the scene—the simple, dimly-lit chapel, the priest, and the two wet and weary animals.
3. Eddi knew and loved the Gospels, and tried to live in their spirit. He preached to the ox and the ass because his Master also had comforted the weak and needy. They were his " brethren ", and had come to the chapel. And Jesus had said :
    Where two or three are gathered together in my name, there am I in the midst of them. (Matthew, xviii, 20.)
4. We like the story because it tells of a simple man, his simple and humble faith, and his love for humble creatures. Such a story is best told simply. The poet has used simple language, and told his tale straight-forwardly from beginning to end. His metre and his arrangement of rhymes are as plain as they can be. He has wished us to think of one thing only, the beauty of Eddi's Service.

*   *   *

<u>A CHRISTMAS CAROL</u> (44)

1. No. All the words are short and simple. We might use every one in our daily speech. The only unusual phrase is " made moan ", and it is very plain.
2. " Stood " means " stood fixed ", " stood without movement or life ". Think how much better the poet's line is than " Earth was hard as iron, " though at first each may seem to say the same thing.
3. (*a*) The lines of the poem are much more vivid. The repetition of " snow on snow " makes us watch the unending fall of the flakes, as it were hour after hour.
   (*b*) The lines of the poem are much softer to say, and snow falls softly. We saw in note 1 that the poet has used simple words ; we also see that simple words, well chosen, may be used to paint the most beautiful pictures.

108

4. " Bleak ".   See notes 2 and 3.   The scene is cheerless without a hint of life, or of welcome to the Baby in the stable.

5. No one can imagine how great God is.   Yet shelter could be found only in a stable for the infant Jesus.

6. No.   In stanza 1 we have been led to look at the frozen scene, and feel the dreary cold.   Line 13 brings this back to us, and we feel much more deeply how poor a shelter a stable must have been, and how lowly was the birth of Jesus.

7. This poem makes us think and feel.   We must, therefore, read it slowly and quietly.   Note how the short lines, (6, 8) help us.   They seem to give us time for thought.

*　　　♣　　　♣

THE FROZEN OCEAN (45)

1. The two pictures are (*a*) of the flowing sea we know, and (*b*) of the frozen ocean into which the poet imagines it wished to change.
The former is restless and " loud " (line 15).   Tides ebb and flow, breakers crash continually, currents and whirlpools are never still.   Ships come and go on the surface and fishes in the depths of the waters.
The latter is still (line 8) and silent (line 22).   Tides and breakers freeze, currents and whirlpools are bound fast.   Where ships came and went foxes step on the ice-fast surface and a solitary bird builds its nest.   These are the only moving things.

2. The picture in " A Christmas Carol " is bleak. (See notes 2, 3 and 4 to that poem.)   The poet has kept all life and colour out of it.   This picture seems bright beside it.   It has living creatures, white foxes, and a bird " coming sweetly ".   The fields of snow rise into mountains of ice.   The moaning wind of the " Carol " is not heard.

3. As you read and re-read the poem, you will discover with what skill the poet has made her lines " pause ", like the sea, and " freeze " into stillness.
In stanza 2 we cannot say the third line quickly if we pronounce each word clearly.   There is a pause, too, in the thought after each pair of words.   Contrast the line with

They lagged and paused and stiffened.

In the fourth line we are forced to pause on " froze ".
In stanza 3 the fourth line again stays our pace.   We must give time to " not ", " old ", and " life ".
In stanza 6 the third line forces us to dwell on " marked ", " join ", " lands' ", " snow ", " fields ", actually five of the eight syllables that compose it.   The fourth line holds us back with its first word, " where ", and we are compelled to dwell on each word in turn :

Where,   no man shall know.

109

1. The poem tells us he was old (line 6) and crinkled (line 22). Were those crinkles due to weather or to merriment? He must have been merry to pipe as he did. The last stanza tells us he was wise, also, for he had seen many, many seasons come and go, and had learned their secrets. Was he an old shepherd (line 6) or a magic piper who looked like a shepherd?

2. He played on a pipe, or reed (line 21) and his tune tripped from it (line 20) a gay little lilt, with notes tumbling fast over each other (line 9). But, gay as it was, it was wise, too, with all the wisdom of the country in it.

3. Have you seen young lambs skipping, with legs that seem too long for their bodies, full of life, but not yet able to jump very far, and every now and again taking little runs? If you have, you will agree that this was an excellent tune for them. Listen to it in the poem:

> *An' they stírred*
>
> *When they héard,*
>
> *Did the líttle young lámbs,*
>
> *Then they hópped, most absúrd,*
>
> *From a-lée of their dáms.*

Beat out the other lines for yourself. The tune has quick, lively " jumps ", quite short jumps, so that even the smallest lambs could keep time to it. Then, at the end of each stanza (lines 10-12, 22-24, 34-36) comes a little run, slow at first, quickening into a " derry down derry ", and ending in a jump.

4. You must form your own opinion. Who was the piper? (See note 1.) The tune did not lead the lambs far away from their mothers, nor did it gather together the wild things of the wold. There is no word of fairies. But was there not magic in the tune that drew the lambs from their shelters and caused them to skip in the cold wind?

5. Little young lambs suggest spring, but those lambs had been born into a very wintry world (lines 1-5). Then the piper came and his gay music told winter to be gone. Think of the gaiety and life of this poem as compared with the stillness of " The Frozen Ocean " (page 45) or the bleakness of " A Christmas Carol " (page 44). " Old Winter " (page 41) is cheerful, but the jollity is that of " lads " cosy within doors, and therefore despising the storm without. In " The Little Young Lambs " we have, instead, the cheerfulness that comes with a first hint of spring.

6. We should remember the lambs, and " skip ". We should read at a brisk pace, and our voices should mark clearly the " beats " and the rhymes. Stanza 3 may be taken more slowly, since it gives us so much to think about. Line 34, especially, will hold us up, partly because it is very difficult to say it quickly, and partly because it puts a very solemn thought before us.

A BIT OF COLOUR (48)

1. " All things were gray ", the scene, the sky, the weather, the carriage, and the clothes of the travellers. Count the number of times the word " gray " is used in lines 1-15. Note, too, the other " gray " words. A " bleak " wind " sobered " everything. The lane was " narrow ", " lonely ", and " old ", surely the very home of " grayness ".

2. (a) There is a world of gray, and only a single flower ; yet it is the tiny bit of yellow that " takes the eye ". The poet painted it in with the last stroke of his brush, so to speak (line 20), and it remains clear in our sight.
(b) The shrill whistle helps us to remember it. The yellow would not have been so bright, had the sweep crouched miserable and dumb.
(c) The flower shines by contrast, against the drab background, like a candle in a dark night. Had the day been blue, and the fields gay with colour, we should probably have failed to see a daffodil even in a sweep's cap.

3. See note 2. " The jaunty air, the sooty face, and the yellow daffodil " were all in welcome contrast to the general dullness. They were cheerful and brave, and promised better things to come. So, when things look black the memory of that morning is still a pleasure and an encouragement.

*   *   *

WHAT THE WEATHER DOES (49)

1. The short, bright lines hint at once that this song is to go with a swing.

The rooks are alive

On the tops of the trees.

By the time we have read four lines, had two rhymes and a " jolly " comparison, we are quite certain that this is a cheerful poem.

2. In this poem we are happy in everything. In " A Bit of Colour " we are happy almost in spite of everything. The poet of the previous poem has used his " gray " brush so heavily that we can see and even feel the east-windy day he describes. Mr. Hamish Hendry does not use colour ; he tells of sounds and brisk movement and leaves us to complete the scene. There is sunshine in his picture, and blue sky. Branches are still leafless, but birds are singing in them ; and it is much more easy to prance in his weather than to whistle with the sooty sweep.

3. The four-line version is much too dull. It stumbles along heavily, with never a hint of spring in its step. The poem dances. It tells us the same things, but tells them in such a way that we seem to be in the sunny air, watching the rooks and hearing their " talk ".

4. We must try to read it with the joy and excitement of the speaker— the child who has been kept prisoner by frost and snow, who comes prancing down the lane, and who would fain fly like the lark in his happiness.

111

THE BLACKBIRD (50)

1. He sings perched on a chimney above the suburbs of a great city.

2. The season is Spring. " He mocks the winter's wrong " (line 13).

3. The poet calls him " my " blackbird, because he thinks of him as an old friend, who in some wonderful way counts the crowded chimneys of the town until he perches always close to the poet's garden. His song is for all who choose to listen, but every listener has full delight in it as though it were for him alone. The blackbird is " bountiful ", that is, liberal, free, generous in his giving. All birds sing generously in Spring, but the bird that brings his music to people in town may especially be described as " bountiful ".

4. Perhaps in line 16. Chimney-pots are hum-drum, common-place, often ugly things. As the song swells above them, they become " celestial ", heavenly. The poet is carried to another and fairer world as he listens.
   In lines 11-12 the same idea is put a little less strongly. The music can make the listener feel that he is back in the country, in a well known wood, all alone with the blackbird.

5. We may arrange the four poems thus :
   (1) " The Little Young Lambs " and " What the Weather Does " ;
   (2) " A Bit of Colour " and " The Blackbird ".
   The poems in the former group express the spirit of Spring-time in the quick movement of their lines. As we read them we feel that Spring is the season of awakening and mirth. The latter pair are more serious. The sooty sweep and the blackbird remain in our memories because they sing in spite of difficulties, and by their " bounty " bring home the joy of Spring to listeners who might have missed it without them.

*   *   *

THE GLASS SHIP (51)

1. Alone among the objects in the shop window, the ship is " complete " (line 5) and " bright " (line 19). It still seems to have work to do (lines 21-22), while for the " hundred huddled things " the time of useful-ness is past. They are dejected, tattered, broken, " dead ". It is " alive ".

2. The children have " envious eyes " (line 25) because they cannot have the ship, but it is good that they should see it. It is good for us all to see beautiful things ; and in order to enjoy them we do not require to possess them. " Dreaming hopes " are fine things, too. The puddled street must appear a far less dingy place to those who hope, however faintly, to find shining ships in its pools.

3. Not so long ago it was the custom to think that only certain subjects were fit for poetry; such subjects as the country with its flowers and trees, the sea with its ships, fairyland with its strange wee folk. Poetry

must be beautiful, and flowers, ships, and fairies are beautiful in them-
selves. Nowadays poets find beauty in things that at first sight may
appear drab and common, and as they make that beauty clear in their
poems we can see it too. We might have passed by the odds and ends
in the dark little window and seen nothing. The poet saw the tiny
ship shining so strangely beside its " gray " companions, like the daffodil
in the sweep's cap (page 48) or the blackbird on the chimney stack
(page 50). She has told us in beautiful and simple words what she saw
and what she felt, and has helped us to share her pleasure.

4. If we use our eyes, as the poet did, we shall see many similar beauties,
even in the dull streets of a city—a flowering plant in a tenement window,
sparrows bathing in a puddle, a pile of oranges in a grocer's window,
a cat sitting at a sunny corner, a little girl nursing her doll in a doorway,
a happy face in a hurrying crowd, a boy helping an old woman at a busy
crossing. You will think of many more.

*   *   *

BLUE STARS AND GOLD (52)

1. The first line and the last two deal with trams and cars. The other
twelve deal with the sky. Nevertheless, lines 1 and 14-15 are very
important. We enjoy the view of the stars all the more because we
know the gazer is looking at them from the street. Note the little
touch of humour in " most awkwardly " (line 14) with which the poet
suddenly brings us back to the street again.

2. It was a still night. There seem to have been no clouds. The air was
" a velvet pall ". Further, as we read the poem, so quietly written
with the still pauses between the stanzas, we somehow *feel* that the
night was calm.

3. The poet himself admits (lines 14-15) that he was not wise to stand
between a car and tram ! But he was surely wise to feast his eyes on all
the beauty of the sky. He has gained a lovely memory, and has shared
its loveliness with us.

4. The titles would not have told us that those were town poems. Indeed,
much of their charm for many of us may come from the contrast
between the subjects and their background. The blackbird and the
starry night are all the more memorable because they are heard or
seen in the city. The glass ship seems to shine more brightly in the
dim shop than it would do, for example, in a cottage by the sea.

5. The poem you are going to make, unlike many you have read,
and like those suggested in note 4 to " The Glass Ship ", will have for
its subject a purely city theme. Think of streams of cars seeming ever
so small and silent from your high window, scurrying past like ants,
each on its own errand.
Note how the poem is built—in stanzas of three lines, each with four
beats, and with the first and third lines rhyming.

113

<u>COUNTRY BUSES</u> (53)

1. The London buses are " stolid " ; they are not free, but must halt or hurry according as the lights are red or green ; the streets are crowded with traffic ; their journeys are " careful ", *i.e.* full of care.
The Country buses are " happy " ; they are " free ", as there are no red or green lights ; the roads have little traffic on them ; they are greeted when they arrive.

2. He is a country man. Note how he loves the country names.

3. When he tells of the passengers in the country buses he speaks as one of them, using always the first person—The country buses link " us " with the villages, serve " our " needs, wait for " us ", are " our " friends, know " us ", know where " we " get down. (You will find more examples in stanza 4.) The London buses, on the other hand, take up a million passengers, but never win " their " hearts.

4. He would probably have talked about the happy London buses, how the red and green lights made the crossings quite safe, how pleasant it was to have the company of all the other traffic, of the endless variety of the people to be seen in them, of the brightly lighted streets even at night, of the good surface, and of the great sights to be seen, *e.g.* St. Paul's, Westminster Abbey, The Tower, The Houses of Parliament. As for the Country buses he would have called them " stolid ", as they went along with no lights to guide them at the crossings, no company, few passengers and generally the same people, while the roads would be lonely and dark at night and often bumpy, and with nothing interesting to be seen.

5. You must decide this for yourself.

6. This is how the buses go :

    The stolid London buses roll down the cars between
or
    ti **tum** *ti ti ti* **tum** *ti ti* **tum** *ti ti ti* **tum**

Note that the four lines of the first stanza all go the same way. But the country buses begin thus :

    But the happy country buses they are free to bowl along
or
    ti ti **tum** *ti ti ti* **tum** *ti ti ti* **tum** *ti ti ti* **tum**

Try the other three lines of the second stanza and you will find there is more variety, that there is more freedom in the rhythm of the country buses. They are not so " stolid ".

You will notice that if you " *ti* tum " the lines of this poem you go fairly fast, but not nearly so fast as you do in the next poem.

7. You would probably have written

   But the happy country buses are free to bowl along,

   instead of

   But the happy country buses they are free to bowl along.

   and so you would have lost the emphasis the poet gives to the country buses.

8. The answer is most clearly shown in

   line 5 : " the happy country buses ",
   line 12 : " the buses are our friends ",
   line 14 : " the kind bus ".

That is, he writes of them as if they were alive, happy and friendly. Of course, he really means the drivers and conductors of the country buses. But his feeling for the men has become a feeling for the bus itself. He feels that it is a happy, kind, friendly bus that is greeted everywhere, that does not charge him much, that waits for him and meets him when he is tired, and takes him home.

*　　*　　*

THE WORLD FROM A RAILWAY CARRIAGE (55)

1. The speaker is in the train ; he is looking out at the world from a railway carriage.

2. It is daytime—forenoon or afternoon.

3. From line 10 we see it is the time for gathering brambles—the end of summer, or early autumn.

4. No. You are in the train looking out at the scenery.

5. Because the train is going so fast, the scene is continually changing, " Each a glimpse and gone for ever ".

6. Bridges and houses, hedges and ditches, the horses and cattle and all of the sights of the hill and the plain.

7. This train goes much faster than the buses. You see, it is a fast train, an " express ". A slow train, a " local ", stops at all the stations. But when you are in this train, " Painted stations whistle by ". In the last poem the buses rumble along. In note 6, above, you saw how they began ; *ti* **tum** *ti ti ti* **tum** *ti, ti* **tum** *ti ti ti* **tum.** But in the train we go off with a rush :

   Faster than fairies, Faster than witches,

   or

   tum *ti ti* **tum** *ti* **tum** *ti ti* **tum** *ti*

115

If you think how a child imitates a train, you might put it thus :

chu chu chu chu chu chu chu chu chu chu

Try it and you will find it goes much faster than the *ti* tum of the buses.

8. The speaker is happy and excited. Have you ever gone down hill on a bicycle ? If so you know the excitement that comes with the speed, what a glorious rush it is.

*   *   *

THE TRAIN (56)

1. In " From a Railway Carriage " the writer is interested in

All of the sights of the hill and the plain

that fly past him as he sits in the train. But Mary Coleridge is standing in the darkness watching the signal lights,

A green eye—and a red—in the dark,

and the train as it comes into sight and sweeps past. She speaks of it as if it were alive, a fierce living thing. In the first eight lines it seems like a fiery dragon rushing through the night.

2. Line 3. " Flashed ". Note that this word not only tells us of the speed of the train, but makes us see its blazing lights as it flashes by.

3. Part 1, lines 1-8, describes the appearance and sound of the train.
   „ 2, lines 9-12, tells us what the train does.
   „ 3, lines 13-16, tells us the effect of its speed.

4. This train goes much faster than the train in the former poem, so fast that places which formerly seemed a long distance apart, because it took a long time to travel from one to the other, now seem close together. In the days of the stage-coach if a man in London wished to visit a friend in Glasgow, it took about a week to go and a week to return. Now he can travel up in one night, spend the day with his friend and travel back in the same way that night. Thus time and space can no longer separate friends. If Mary Coleridge were living now she would have written her poem about an aeroplane.

5. No ! In the last poem we were in the train, travelling with it and we could not help hearing and feeling the beat, the rhythm. Here we simply see it flash by and hear the thunder of its motion.

6. No. When the teacher gives a command, it is short and exact. If he said, " I want you all to stand up," you might not understand at first, but when he says, " All Stand," you jump to your feet. This is the effect of the short last line. Do you not feel as if you were actually watching the train disappear in the darkness ? In the last short line it suddenly fades out as if it had gone round a curve.

116

7. In " From a Railway Carriage " you were in the train, enjoying the speed and watching the scenery hurry past. In this poem you are standing alone in the silence and the dark, and the train appears like a living monster. Note that the signal lights are not

A green light—and a red—in the dark

but

A green eye—and a red—in the dark.

The train itself is a " wild thing ", " rushing, tearing thro' the night ", shattering " her silence with shrieks ". The silence has come back at the end of the poem.

The first poem reminds us of a person happy and excited, running very fast but with short steps ; the second seems to rush through the night with long bounds. The manner in which stanza 1 is printed emphasises this, gives the feeling of breathless speed.

*　　　*　　　*

BORDER MARCH (57)

1. Yes. His poem is a March. When soldiers with their band are marching through the streets, you will notice two things about the music ; (*a*) it is loud, for all the soldiers must hear it ; (*b*) the time or beat is very clearly marked—so clearly that you cannot help keeping time to it as you follow the band.

2. (*a*) The beat is so definite, so marked in this poem that when we read it aloud we cannot help emphasising it. Read the first eight lines of " The Train ", then the first stanza of this poem and you will hear the difference.

   (*b*) Some of the words sound loud. Take the first word, " March ". Say the three words : " manse ", " marsh ", " march ". " Marsh " is louder than " manse ", while " march " is not only still louder, but it ends so sharply that it sounds like a bark. In the first four lines, this word occurs five times. There are other loud words, but you can find them for yourselves.

   (*c*) Sometimes two or more words in the same line begin with the same consonant (alliteration),

   All the Blue Bonnets are bound for the border.

   Compare with this the last line :

   When the Blue Bonnets came over the border,

   and you feel that " over " is not nearly so loud as " bound ". Line 13 is a fine example of how alliteration helps the sound :

   Come to the crag where the beacon is blazing.

   (*d*) A rhyme like " order ", " border " (lines 2 and 4) is called double rhyme and always helps the sound. There are many more examples of this in the poem.

117

3. Yes. The short lines are better for two reasons :
(*a*) They make the rhymes, " spread ", " head ", and " then ", " glen ", sound more clearly, because they are each at the end of a line.
(*b*) The change from the long four-beat line to the short two-beat line gives variety, seems to add spirit to the poem, giving a sort of jaunty effect.

4. How do you feel when you are marching after a band ? Do you not feel confident, a little excited, inclined to hold your head up and square your shoulders ? This is how the speaker feels. He is looking forward to a successful raid, perhaps thinking of plunder, at any rate confident of victory.
Here is a stanza from another march. Read it aloud.

> *Kentish Sir Byng stood for his King,*
> *Bidding the crop-headed Parliament swing :*
> *And, pressing a troop, unable to stoop*
> *And see the rogues flourish and honest folk droop,*
> *Marched them along, fifty-score strong,*
> *Great-hearted gentlemen, singing this song.*
>
> *From* " Cavalier Tunes " by Browning.

*   *   *

THE SONG OF THE WESTERN MEN (58)

1. The feeling running through the poem is one of defiance, together with confidence either that they will set Trelawny free or avenge his death. But this springs from their love of Trelawny and loyalty to him.

2. The challenge in its definite form is given twice in the poem and in almost the same words—in the last two lines of stanzas 2 and 6. But in reality it is given six times in the poem. The last two lines of every stanza are a challenge and, though different in words, practically the same challenge.

3. In each poem there is the same confidence of victory, the same feeling of excitement. But this poem is more personal. In " Border March " there is the excitement of an attack on the usual enemy—the English. But here there is anger that Trelawny has been sent to the Tower, and determination to free him or avenge his death. And they are to fight against their own king. There is more eagerness and joy in " Border March ". Here there is more grim determination, the poem is one long defiance. Read the two poems aloud and you will find your manner of reading changes as you pass from the one to the other.

4. Because it is love for Trelawny and loyalty to him that fires their spirit. Notice that their love is never mentioned in the poem, yet it is so evident in it and so strong that we cannot help being on their side. This is the most beautiful thing in the poem and all the more beautiful because it is not mentioned.

1. Take the Song first :

> Now we are the rodent mariners,
> As nobody needs be told,
> For there's no mistaking our nautical airs,
> Our rolling eyes and bold ;
> And 'tis never a ship leaves English ground
> From Liverpool Docks to Plymouth Sound,
> For San Francisco or Bombay bound,
> But we have the run of her hold.

Look at the shape of this stanza. The first four lines consist of long and short lines alternately, the number of beats being 4, 3, 4, 3. After this we half expect another 4, 3, but what we get is 4, 4, 4, 3, and because we have been expecting the short three-beat line, it is very welcome and satisfactory when it comes. In addition, the rhymes absolutely support the effect of the rhythm ; for they begin alternately, " mariners ", " told ", " airs ", " bold ", and then, as in the rhythm, we have " ground ", " sound ", " bound ", " hold " ; and " hold " not only takes us back to the three-beat line, but it rhymes with " told " and " bold ". This sounds very dry, but, if you have worked it out, read these eight lines aloud again, and you will feel the swing and " go ", and hear the rhyme, and understand why the poet called it a song. Now take the next four lines :

> With a pit-a-pit pat
> And a chip chip chip,
> 'Tis the brown sea rat
> That is captain of the ship !

Well, what has happened now ? Don't you agree that it sounds as if the rats had begun to dance ? Don't you see them skipping along, pit-a-pit pat and chip, chip, chip, just as in that old dance, the polka ? You may think of this poem as a rat concert and dance, and you will notice they get a good dance at the end. What happens in the last four lines ? Do they just dance on, or do you see the rats all scuttling away to their holes, with a " ho ho ho ", so that the last you hear of them is, " We are masters of the main " ?

2. We should prefer to share the feast of the Brown Sea Rat. We could enjoy everything in it. Could you enjoy everything in the other feast ?

1. Lines 33 and 34 certainly seem to refer to an old man :

> *"P'raps," and he'd smooth his hairless mouth,*
> *"P'raps, if 'twere now, my son."*

But the whole manner of telling the story reminds us of an old man speaking of his young days.

2. We are not told, but we feel that he still lives in the same house as he did when he was young. He may be an old fisherman who has spent his life in the one place.

3. We are not told definitely, but everything suggests that he is telling his story looking out into the bay where he saw the mermaid.

4. He tells his story slowly, quietly, earnestly.

Slowly.—Before Sam begins to speak the poem goes slow. Read the first four lines and notice how you want to pause at " shingle " in line 3 and " foam " in line 4, and then roll out the next word so that you hear every syllable :

> *Breaks on the shingle, emerald-green,*
> *In white foam, endlessly.*

Sam is trying to make his hearer see each picture, because, if you do not believe and see each one in turn, you will neither believe in nor see the mermaid. We have four pictures.

(*a*) The small boy leaning from his window in the moonlight watching the waves.

(*b*) The hands and eyes he saw sparkling in the waves as they broke in the moonlight.

(*c*) The loneliness of the immense stretch of the moonlit sea.

(*d*) The mermaid.

You could not imagine him hurrying.

Quietly.—This is one of the quietest of poems—so quiet that Sam at the window can hear the mermaid calling from the sea, though her call is half a whisper.

> *Calling me, "Sam !" —quietlike—"Sam !"*

You notice he takes the trouble to tell us she called " quietlike ". You may say—" But what about all these breaking waves he paints so wonderfully, do they make no noise ? " Well, do you *hear* them in the poem ?

That is what seems so wonderful—we cannot hear them. It is a beautiful, moonlit, silent picture with a voice from the waves, half whispering, calling—quietlike—" Sam ". It is because Sam was so accustomed to the sound of the waves that he did not seem to hear them ; and so, when he tells the story, we do not hear them either.

Earnestly.—He is entirely in earnest, for this is the most wonderful experience in his life, the one thing his memory goes back to, as the first line of the poem tells us. Indeed, he is so much in earnest that we believe him, we see that wonderful moonlit silent sea, the magic of its breaking waves, feel the immense loneliness, and then,

> *All in the solitudinous sea*
> *Of that there lonely bay*

we see the mermaid, hear her calling, *"Sam ! "—quietlike—"Sam ! "*.

5. Read again lines 6-17 and you will find that line 17 seems to wake you up, bring you back to yourself. In the same way everything was calling Sam away, the moonlight, the sea, the tiny hands and eyes, like sparks of frost, the loneliness, " Just ocean there and me ", and then he hears his father snore and that brings him back to himself and his home. Perhaps that is why he did not go when the mermaid called.

*   *   *

THE LOWLANDS OF HOLLAND (64)

1. We should like to know :

   (*a*) Why did her love go to Holland ? Was it on business, or in war, or simply for adventure ?

   (*b*) Did the first ship sink, and if so, did she run on a rock, or sink in a storm, or was she sunk in battle ?

   (*c*) Does the third line simply mean that the ship sank and six score mariners went with her ?

   (*d*) How did her love and his twenty mariners escape ?

2. No ! It is true that we are not definitely told either that the ship sank or that her lover and his mariners were drowned. But lines 7 and 8 are so full of fate that we know. Note the strange effect of the adjective in " weary wind ". It is not the wind that is weary, but the lady that is weary of the sound of the wind, and she makes us feel that it is a fatal wind. Then the ship turned withershins, that is, the opposite way of the sun—from west to east—a sure sign of doom.

3. Because she is not interested in telling us a story. She is lamenting the death of her lover. Had he escaped she might have told us all about his adventures. But what did his escape in the first journey matter, now that he was drowned ? Note how much more powerful the second stanza is. The first stanza, in which she tells of the first journey, is practically a list of facts. But the second, which tells of the death of her lover, is a tragic picture.

121

4. You must decide for yourself. But you must not, as some people do, blame the mother for being hard-hearted. She loves her daughter and wishes to cheer her up, to keep her from pining away.

* * *

THE TARRY BUCCANEER (65)

1. He is a small boy, younger than you are. The second last line shows us this most clearly. He is going to be a terrible pirate, you see, and his flag is to be " the wickedest that ever flew ".

2. No. He wishes to be captain of the tarry buccaneers.

3. He has a sash of crimson velvet, a diamond-hilted sword, a silver whistle hanging round his neck by a gold cord, a spy-glass tucked beneath his arm, and a cocked hat. Note it is not only a cocked hat, but it is cocked askew, and there is a silver flagon full of red wine waiting for him. Is he not a fine fellow and does not the picture come straight from some picture book for children ?
Now for the ship.—She is a long, low rakish schooner, with a bright brass pivot-gun, flying the " skull and crossbones ".—Complete the picture for yourself.

4. You would take four steps to each line, thus :

I'm going to be a pirate with a bright brass pivot-gun,

And an island in the Spanish Main beyond the setting sun,

And a silver flagon full of red wine to drink when work is done,

Like a fine old salt-sea scavenger, like a tarry Buccaneer.

* * *

THE VAGABOND (66)

1. Yes, he is quite contented, more than contented, for he feels he is better off than other men, " lord of a dozen counties ", and " with never a care to carry ".

2. His home is the dozen counties. He has no house ; he sleeps in the open, as we see in lines 9-10.

3. He knows them and loves them better than anyone else and he roams about them as he pleases.

4. No and yes.

5. You would not like to be a rolling stone, with no home, sleeping in the open even in winter. But read lines 1-4 and 9-12 carefully. We should all love to have that intimate knowledge of the countryside, to know the stars and the song of the wind as he does. But more than all, we should like to have that contentment in the abundance of his " wealth " that we see in the lines,

> *But I've a treasure that's never spent,*
> *I'm lord of a dozen counties.*

6. " The Lowlands of Holland " goes slowly and sadly as a lament should; there is no variation in the number of beats in each line ; it goes like a solemn march. In " The Vagabond ", lines 1-4 have each four beats and there is a steady swing in them. He is speaking earnestly of what he loves. But lines 5-8 go four-beat, three-beat, four-beat, three-beat, and they go with a lilt as if the vagabond had tossed his cap in the air and begun to caper about for pure light-heartedness.

*　　　*　　　*

HIE AWAY (67)

1. Lines 3-8.
These six lines all begin with the word " where ", yet we do not feel that it is repeated too often. Lines 1-2 invite us away ; then we are given a list of the beautiful spots we are to see—where-where-where, and this gives a feeling of eagerness to the lines. Notice also that in these lines the rhymes are all double : " greenest ", " sheenest ", etc.
Lines 11-12.
These are just the first two lines over again, but the order is changed. If you were anxious to get your companions to go with you to see a Punch and Judy show, wouldn't you call to them, " Come on ; there's a big crowd yonder and I can hear the Punch and Judy man. Come on." In the same way the speaker in the poem calls, " Hie away," then tells you what you will see and finishes with " Hie away ".

2. You must choose for yourself. Many prefer :

> *Hie to haunts right seldom seen,*
> *Lovely , lonesome, cool, and green.*

They remind us of two lines from another poem (" Kubla Khan ") :

> *And here were forests ancient as the hills,*
> *Enfolding sunny spots of greenery.*

3. The vagabond tells us of the beautiful spots he knows and exults in his
   freedom. The speaker here invites us to come with him to see all the
   beautiful spots. There is an eagerness in his invitation that we cannot
   resist, and a love of beauty, of all things " lovely, lonesome, cool, and
   green ".

*   *   *

IN SUMMER TIME (68)

1. He is one of the dancers, one of the country folk, though we do not
   know his name.

2. The pleasures of the country folk in summer time, especially their jolly
   dances in the open air, " under the greenwood tree ".

3. The rhythm—four-beat, three-beat, alternately—goes with a dancing
   swing, especially in lines 7-8 and 15-16.
   The rhymes are peculiar and interesting. Note, for instance, the mid-
   rhymes : " Moll ", " Doll " ; " whisk it ", " frisk it " ; " skip it ",
   " trip it ". Again, in the first stanza, we have " tree ", " we ",
   " Bettee ", " tree ", all rhyming.
   Think of the charming picture—summer time, flowers springing, birds on
   the trees, old Hal playing his pipe while the young folk dance in the
   greenwood.
   The speaker is entirely happy, not in the least envious of lords and
   knights. Everything is in tune with the light-hearted spirit of the poem.

*   *   *

CARGOES (69)

1. Three ships : one with five banks of oars for stanza 1, a Spanish galleon
   in sail for stanza 2, a small steam ship for stanza 3.

2. The cargoes. They would be stored below in the hold.

3. Because in this poem the cargo seems to be the heart or spirit of each
   ship, so much so that if we change the cargo, we feel that in some strange
   way the ship is changed also :

> *Stately Spanish galleon coming from the Isthmus,*
> *Dipping through the Tropics by the palm-green "bays ",*
> *With a cargo of Tyne coal,*
> *Road-rails, pig-lead,*
> *Firewood, iron-ware, and cheap tin trays.*

What has become of our picture ? Of course the galleon could not
have had such a cargo, as many of the things were not invented, but

124

put in similar things that suit the times and you will still find that your picture of the ship could not carry them. Our stately Spanish galleon would not be right, even if she carried a cargo of ivory, apes and peacocks. Somehow she is no longer stately. If you wish to make a really comic picture, you have merely to change one of the other cargoes, thus :

> *Dirty British coaster with a salt-caked smoke-stack,*
> *Butting through the Channel in the mad March "time ",*
> *With a cargo of ivory,*
> *And apes and peacocks,*
> *Sandalwood, cedarwood, and sweet white wine.*

4. You may say that there is nothing in the stanza to indicate the weather, that it may have been a grey sullen day with wind and rain, but you know that when you painted your picture of the quinquireme, you showed her rowing along in beautiful, peaceful, sunny weather over a blue sea. And you were right ; for that is the spirit of the stanza ; and we get it from the cargo. Ivory and apes and peacocks ! you would not naturally think of them in the rain.

5. No, Mr. Masefield is a lover of ships and knows them as we shall never know them. If he had wished a beautiful modern ship for his third picture, he could easily have found one. But he calls his poem " Cargoes ", not " Ships ". The third cargo consists of things we know and are familiar with. They are all for use, not beauty, and we could not do without some of them. So they come in a ship meant for use, not beauty. Yet if you paint your picture well, especially remembering the line :

> *Butting through the Channel in the mad March days,*

your third picture will have a wild beauty, and, somehow, a spirit of courage in the little coaster butting her way through the huge waves.

6. Probably to Solomon :

> *For the king had at sea a navy of Tharshish with the navy of*
> *Hiram : once in three years came the navy of Tharshish,*
> *bringing gold, and silver, ivory, and apes, and peacocks.*
>
> (I Kings, x, 22.)

Do you notice that Mr. Masefield has taken the exact words of the Bible, " ivory, and apes, and peacocks " ?

1. It reminds us of the Quinquireme of Nineveh with its apes and peacocks and ivory. See "Cargoes", page 69, and note 6, page 125. Again in I Kings, x, 11-12, we find the following :

> *And the navy also of Hiram, that brought gold from Ophir, brought in from Ophir great plenty of almug trees, and precious stones. And the king made of the almug trees pillars for the house of the Lord, and for the king's house, harps also and psalteries for singers : there came no such almug trees, nor were seen unto this day.*

2. We realise it in line 3, when we discover that the rhyme for "ivory" is "why for he". This is a good "comic" rhyme, but you could not imagine it in a serious poem. See also stanza 3, lines 27, 29, where "King o' Tyre" rhymes with "ring, attire". Some of the other rhymes are very beautiful, such as the double rhymes in lines 31-33, "slipping", "dipping", "dripping", and again in line 38, "skipping". Read stanza 3 aloud and you will feel the effect of these rhymes.

3. The poem does not say so. In line 15 we are told that Solomon was :

> *Seeking wisdom of earth and air,*

that is, he was seeking to understand the ways of nature, just as scientists are still doing. Of all the animals none look so wise as the apes. You must have seen that for yourself, if you have ever been to a menagerie. You sometimes feel they could speak if they wished. So Solomon wished to understand them, but :

> *If he asked them, they'd only scratch.*

4. If you read I Kings, v, 1-9, you will learn that "Hiram was ever a lover of David", Solomon's father, and that he became a friend to Solomon. Also he was a "merchant chief", a practical man, wise in the ways of the world.

5. People sometimes say in jest that monkeys could speak if they wished, but that they are too wise to do so ; because, if they did, men would teach them and make them work. So they just look wise and say nothing.

> *And " 'Tis excellent knowledge," King Hiram said,*
> *" That keeps its learning inside its head."*

It looks as if Hiram thought just as we do about the monkeys.

1. This poem comes at the end of the story, " Kaa's Hunting ", in " The Jungle Book ". In this story the Bandar-log, the monkey people, steal away the little boy, Mowgli, who lives with the animals of the jungle ; and his friends Baloo, the bear, and Bagheera, the black panther, persuade Kaa, the big python, to join them in hunting the Bandar-log.

   When the monkeys are shifting from one part of the jungle to another, their road lies not on the ground, but through the high trees. It is a wonderful sight to see them swinging and leaping from branch to branch, and tree to tree.

2. In " The Jungle Book " the monkeys are not regarded in the same way as Solomon regards **them** in the last poem. The other animals treat them as the outcasts of the jungle, and refuse to take any notice of them. They chatter so much about the great things they are going to do, but never do them, as they are always changing their minds. This is the explanation of line 7 in each stanza.

<blockquote>
Now you're angry but . . .
Now we're going to . . .   ⎫ What ? Never mind.
Let's pretend we are . . .
</blockquote>

   And so they add their little joke, always the same :

   Brother, thy tail hangs down behind !

3. Many prefer the rhythm, the way it goes, the fine swing in the lines that helps us to see the leaping monkeys. Stanzas 1-3 are a real song for the monkeys, while in the last four long lines they are away, leaping and swinging through the trees.

*   *   *

GOLLYWOG (73)

1. The speaker is a very young boy or girl, probably not old enough yet to come to school.

2. Yes. It gives a fine effect of emphasis. You see he is accusing Gollywog of doing various things, and each " who " comes with something like a thud. When you are caught doing something wrong and the person says, " Who did that ? " he is not really asking a question, he is practically saying, " You did that." Now read the two stanzas and you will find that each " who " seems to drive things further home ; each " who " seems to say to Gollywog, " You did it ". " You did it ".

3. It would make a serious difference. The poem is to be about Gollywog, and we feel his importance much more, when he gets a line to himself. Again the rhymes get more emphasis at the end of the line, because we tend always to make a slight pause there. But perhaps the most important difference is in the rhythm. In the way it is printed in the question, stanza 1 goes four-beat, three-beat, four-beat, three-beat. But this is exactly the same as stanza 2. As the poet has put it, we have much more variety, thus :

> Stanza 1 : 2, 2, 3, 2, 2, 3 (beats).
> Stanza 2 : 4, 3, 4, 3, 4, 3, 4, 3 (beats).

4. Well ! well ! it could not be Gollywog, so it must be the speaker himself. The most amusing thing in the poem is that he does not see it. He knows all the bad things that have been done and that Gollywog was alone there.

> *Gollywog did it, there isn't a doubt—*
> *Nobody else was there.*

How does he know then ? Isn't he a little imp ? But he is so young and so amusing that you cannot help liking him.

*   *   *

THE PIED PIPER OF HAMELIN (77)

1. In stanza II he tells us what a pest the rats were, by giving us a list of all the things they did—" fought the dogs "—" killed the cats "—" bit the babies "—" ate the cheeses "—" licked the soup "—" split open the kegs of salted sprats "—and we are beginning to feel how terrible it all is, when he gives it a humorous turn, with :

> *Made nests inside men's Sunday hats,*
> *And even . . .*

These two words make us expect the climax, the most terrible thing of all, but we get :

> *And even spoiled the women's chats.*

This is called an anticlimax and the effect here is very amusing. You should try to bring this out in your reading.

In stanza VII, lines 106-118, he tells us of the gathering of the rats.

Listen to the noise growing and growing, and note how the rhymes help it in these lines :

> *And ere three shrill notes the pipe uttered,*
> *You heard as if an army muttered ;*
> *And the muttering grew to a grumbling ;*
> *And the grumbling grew to a mighty rumbling ;*
> *And out of the houses the rats came tumbling,*

128

The word " tumbling " comes almost like an explosion. Don't you see the rats pouring out of the houses from every corner—doors, windows, stairs, cellars, etc. ? Now read the list of the rats and watch the rhymes :

> *Great rats, small rats, lean rats, brawny rats,*
> *Brown rats, black rats, grey rats, tawny rats,*
> *Grave old plodders, gay young friskers,*
> > *Fathers, mothers, uncles, cousins,*
> *Cocking tails and pricking whiskers,*
> > *Families by tens and dozens.*

Well surely that is every rat now. No !

> *Brothers, sisters, husbands, wives*
> *Followed the Piper for their lives.*

Don't you feel, as the Americans put it, that you have got every last rat ? That is a real climax.

2. The first nine lines run smoothly and quietly, and then comes line 10, a single word—" Rats ! " This is a real explosion ; it startles us as if someone had shrieked. You see it has a whole line to itself and is followed by an exclamation mark.

3. You must choose for yourself. What do you think of lines 139-142 : " Munch on ", " crunch on ", " nuncheon ", " luncheon ", " puncheon ", " sun shone " ?
For a treble rhyme you have " brawny rats ", " tawny rats "; and for a rhyme even longer, " by psaltery ", " drysaltery ".

4. See " Song of the Brown Sea Rat ", note 2, page 119.

INDEX OF FIRST LINES

	Page
A good sword and a trusty hand	58
A green eye—and a red—in the dark	56
Alas, my Love ! you do me wrong	28
Allen-a-Dale has no fagot for burning	26
Apes and peacocks and almug and ivory	70
As I was walking all alone	30
Beside the blaze of forty fires,	34
Dreary lay the long road, dreary lay the town	20
Eddi, priest of St. Wilfrid	42
Faster than fairies, faster than witches	55
Gollywog	73
Gray was the morn, all things were gray	48
Hamelin Town's in Brunswick	77
He blinks upon the hearth-rug	40
He comes on chosen evenings	50
Here we go in a flung festoon	72
Hie away, hie away	67
If ye fear to be affrighted	35
If ye will with Mab find grace	35
I heard a horseman	34
I know the pools where the grayling rise	66
I'm going to be a pirate with a bright brass pivot-gun	65
I now collected all the stragglers I could find	21
In the bleak mid-winter	44
In the fold	46
In the morning when ye rise	35
In Summer time, when flowers do spring	68
I see it daily as I pass	51
It's pleasant in Holy Mary	16

March, march, Ettrick and Teviotdale 57
My love he's built a bonnie ship, and set her on the sea . . . 64
Now we are the rodent mariners 59
Old Winter sad, in snow yclad 41
One hundred and twenty years ago 36
Quinquireme of Nineveh 69
So the foemen have fired the gate, men of mine 24
The rooks are alive 49
The sea would flow no longer 45
The stolid London buses roll down the cars between 53
The tortoiseshell cat 39
They live 'neath the curtain 32
This made me think upon that miraculous passage in Hamelen . . 74
Three jolly Farmers 10
What is the sound, little brother 38
When I was young, I had no sense 14
When Sam goes back in memory 62
While thus in peaceful guise they sate 17
While walking through the trams and cars 52
Will you gang to the Highlands, Leezie Lindsay 26